God on the Hill

God on the Hill

Temple Poems from Tirupati

Annamayya

TRANSLATED BY

Velcheru Narayana Rao
and David Shulman

OXFORD
UNIVERSITY PRESS

2005

OXFORD
UNIVERSITY PRESS

Oxford University Press, Inc., publishes works that further
Oxford University's objective of excellence
in research, scholarship, and education.

Oxford New York
Auckland Cape Town Dar es Salaam Hong Kong Karachi
Kuala Lumpur Madrid Melbourne Mexico City Nairobi
New Delhi Shanghai Taipei Toronto

With offices in
Argentina Austria Brazil Chile Czech Republic France Greece
Guatemala Hungary Italy Japan Poland Portugal Singapore
South Korea Switzerland Thailand Turkey Ukraine Vietnam

Published by Oxford University Press, Inc.
198 Madison Avenue, New York, New York 10016

www.oup.com

Library of Congress Cataloging-in-Publication Data
Tallapaka Annamacharya, 1408-1503.
[Selections. English. 2005]
God on the hill: temple poems from Tirupati/Annamayya; translated by Velcheru Narayana Rao
and David Shulman.
p. cm.
In English: translated from Telugu.
Includes bibliographical references and index.
ISBN-13 978-0-19-518283-5; 978-0-19-518284-2 (pbk.)
ISBN 0-19-518283-9; 0-19-518284-7 (pbk.)
I. Narayanaravu, Velcheru, 1932– II. Shulman, David Dean, 1949– III. Title.

PL4780.9.T25A24 2005
894.8'2712—dc22 2004065419

1 3 5 7 9 8 6 4 2
Printed in the United States of America
on acid-free paper

FOR THE GOD ON THE HILL AT TIRUPATI

yat karoṣi yad aśnāsi yaj juhoṣi dadāsi yat
yat tapasyasi kaunteya tat kuruṣva mad-arpaṇam

Preface

Tāḷḷapāka Annamayya or Annamâcārya, who lived at the great hilltop shrine of Tirupati in south India, in Andhra Pradesh, in the fifteenth century, is said to have composed a song a day for the god of this temple, Veṅkaṭeśvara-Vishṇu. Late in his lifetime or, possibly, not long after his death, some thirteen thousand of these poems, all in the *padam* genre, were inscribed on copper plates and stored in a special vault inside the temple. The hagiographical tradition of Tirupati asserts that this surviving corpus is less than half of Annamayya's original oeuvre. These poems are the Tirupati temple's greatest treasure.

The language of the poems is Telugu—one of the classical languages of south India and a major vehicle for the texts of the Carnatic musical tradition. Annamayya's poems were meant to be sung, although the precise, original manner of singing them fell into disuse and has only recently been partially reconstructed. The poet himself indicated the *rāga* in which each poem was to be sung, as we see from the copper plates. The standard *padam* format includes an opening line or lines, *pallavi*, followed by three *caraṇam* verses, each of which returns to the *pallavi* refrain. The *padam* is thus a highly integrated, internally resonant syntactic and thematic unit.

Annamayya's poems were editorially divided—already in the copper plates—into two major categories, *śṛṅgāra* ("erotic") and *adhyātma* ("metaphysical"). The former, which comprise nearly three-quarters of the entire surviving corpus, deal with the infinite varieties and nuances of the god's love life, which the poet knows intimately. Usually these poems are couched in the female voice. So-called *adhyātma* poems are, by way of contrast, sung in the poet's own voice and deal with his sense of himself as an agonized, turbulent human being in relation to the god he worships. These two categories are superbly complementary; taken together, they explore and articulate a wide range of human experience. In that sense, they are universal poems that speak to all of us.

Acknowledgments

We are indebted to the great scholars who edited and published the Annamayya corpus from the copper plates in Tirupati in the course of the twentieth century: Veturi Prabhakara Sastri, Rallapalli Anantakrishna Sarma, Arcakam Udayagiri Srinivasacaryulu, and Gauripeddi Ramasubbasarma. We, in particular, wish to thank Arcakam Udayagiri Srinivasacaryulu for the depth of his insights and for sharing his memories with us directly.

We cite the *padams* first by copper plate number (CP), preceded by A (*adhyātma*) or S (*śṛṅgāra*), and then by volume and page number in the 1998–99 photo-reprinting of the entire Annamayya corpus by the Tirumala-Tirupati Devasthanams (twenty-nine volumes). Joyce B. Flueckiger and P. C. Narasimha Reddy kindly sent us each a complete set of the volumes.

Contents

Note on Selection and Translation

We have read through the Annamayya corpus over a period of some years, occasionally translating some *padams* that caught our imagination wherever we happened to find ourselves—in Madison, Jerusalem, Berlin, Oxford, North Carolina, Heidelberg; on trains, airplanes, sometimes even at home. A few early translations were done together with our dear friend, A. K. Ramanujan, and were included in our volume, *When God Is a Customer.* We have incorporated a few of these in the present volume.

Our selection of poems for translation was largely guided by considerations of translatability and poetic interest. We picked poems we felt were both strong in their own right and representative of major themes and voices. The volume is meant to provide a small sample—less than 1 percent of the surviving poems—that may serve to suggest something of the variety and the vitality of this tradition. We have freely interspersed "metaphysical" and "erotic" *padams;* the two genres are clearly meant to resonate with each other. With a little practice, the reader should soon easily identify the transition from female to male voice as one translated *padam* leads into the next.

In performance, singers normally return to the *pallavi* refrain after performing each *caraṇam*-verse of a *padam*. Rather than repeating the entire two-line *pallavi,* we have, in most cases, chosen a significant phrase from it in order to reproduce in translation something of the effect of the refrain. In some poems in which repetition is built into the *caraṇam* verses, or in cases where we felt repetition was not helpful to the poem, we have not given a refrain. Our task was to transform a sung poem into a readable poem, and this aim has guided our work throughout.

We have opted for simple diction that would reflect the lyrical qualities of the original. Annamayya's language was a relatively simple, fifteenth-century Telugu, close to spoken rhythms, in any case immediately intelligible to a listener of that time. By now, some five centuries later, certain lexical usages have become opaque. No tradition of commentary exists for these poems, nor have modern Telugu lexicographers paid the corpus much attention. As a result, at times we have had to make our own interpretations based on our judgment and experience. We have tried to preserve the tone and texture of the original as faithfully as possible. If some of the translations sound too modern to the reader, we want to reassure him or her that in no case have we strayed far from the connotations and meanings of the original. Annamayya's "modernity" is one of the surprising features of this corpus and might make us want to rethink the question of when a "modern" sensibility began to emerge in south India.

An afterword explores at some length the historical, religious, and poetic contexts and themes linked to Annamayya's poems. We recommend, however, that you turn first to the texts themselves and let them speak or sing.

God on the Hill

The Poems

Tell him this one thing.
Distant rivers always reach the sea.

Being far is just like being near.
Would I think of him if I were far?
The sun in the sky is very far from the lotus.
From a distance, friendship is intense.

Distant rivers reach the sea.

The moment he looks at me, I look back at him.
My face is turned only toward him.
Clouds are in the sky, the peacock in the forest.
Longing is in the look that connects.

Distant rivers reach the sea.

To speak of desire is as good as coming close.
Haven't I come close to him?
The god on the hill is on the hill,
and where am I?
Look, we made love.
Miracles do happen.

Distant rivers reach the sea.

SCP 259, 9:29
vibhunikin ī māṭe vinnaviñcarā

Why cross the boundary
when there is no village?
It's like living without a name,
like words without love.

What use is ecstasy
without the agony of separation?
Shade is nothing without the burning sun.
What is patience without fury of passion?
Why make anything—love or poetry—if two can't be one?

Why cross the boundary?

What good is profit without praise?
Why speak tender words when there is no closeness?
What use is love if you can't let go?
Beauty is empty without desire.

Why cross the boundary?

Why have a lover you don't need to hide?
Intimacy is dull without doubt.
What fun is there in just making love,
no extras, no questions?
Bring in our god on the hill.

Why cross the boundary?

SCP 9, 5:38
ūru leni pŏlimera peru pĕmpu leni bratuku

You say you want to bathe
when the waves subside.
Is there an end
to the endless mind?

You say, "Let me quench my thirst,
and then I'll find the truth."
Why should thirst be quenched?
How can you know truth?

Is there an end?

All the days you have a body,
why should longing cease?
How can you find joy?

Is there an end?

You say, "After I know what lies ahead,
I'll forget what was before."
Can you know what lies ahead?
How can you forget what was before?

Is there an end?

That goodness that comes of knowing
how to reach god—
you won't find it
in your wildest dreams.

Is there an end?

ACP 36, 1:150
kaḍal uḍipi nīr āḍagā dalacuvāralaku

Seeing is one thing,
looking is another.
If both come together,
that is god.

If you look for an elephant,
he comes as an elephant.
If you look for a tree,
he's a tree.
If you look for a mountain,
he'll be a mountain.
God is what you have in your mind.

If you look for empty space,
he appears as space.
If you look for an ocean,
he'll be an ocean.
If you look for a city,
he will come as a city.
God is what you have in your mind.

If you think of the god on the hill,
married to the goddess,
that's who you'll see.
What you look for
is the god in you.
What you see
is the god out there.
God is what you have in your mind.

ACP 134, 2:95
cūce cūp' ŏkaṭi sūṭi guriy yŏkaṭi

When I'm done being angry,
then I'll make love.
Right now, you should be glad
I'm listening.

When you flash that big smile,
I smile back. It doesn't mean I'm not angry.
You keep looking at me,
so I look, too. It isn't right
to ignore the boss.

Right now you should be glad.

You say something, and I answer.
That doesn't make it a conversation.
You call me to bed, I don't make a fuss.
But unless I want it myself,
it doesn't count as love.

Right now you should be glad.

You hug me, I hug you back.
You can see I'm still burning.
I can't help it, god on the hill,
if I'm engulfed in your passion.

Right now you should be glad.

SCP 1617, 26:78
kopamu dīrina mīda gūḍe gāni

I'll serve you as best I can,
but some things I just can't do.

I can melt your heart just like that,
but I can't stop you breaking out in sweat.
I can sink my teeth deep into your lips,
but I can't help it if they leave marks.

Some things I just can't do.

I can touch you where you are shy,
but can I stop you from feeling the thrill?
I can look you straight in the eyes,
but hey, can I keep you
from smiling?

Some things I just can't do.

I can wear you out with hugs and kisses,
but I can't stop your sigh.
Now that you've made love to me,
god on the hill,
can I keep you from wanting more?

Some things I just can't do.

SCP 260, 9:35
cetanaina pāṭi seva seyudu gāka

I study just for the day,
forgetting as I learn.

They used to study
to find God.
Now we study
to forget him.

Study just for the day.

In the age of the beginning, people read
to know him truly.
In our dying age, we read only
to deny him.

Study just for the day.

The masters among the gods
sought knowledge so they could get him.
Today's experts
seek money to forget him.

Study just for the day.

ACP 15, 1:63
nāṭiki nāḍe nā caduvu

When you're done with one puppet,
another will be waiting.
Life is a play of shadows on the screen.

If you get rid of poverty, you're stuck with riches.
You'll never have time to think of god.
There's always a zillion things to do.
Life whips you, like a bonded slave,

this play of shadows on the screen.

If you say no to bad things, you are bound by the good.
You'll never have time to think of god.
Life seeps in, like water under the carpet.
If you won't work for wages, it'll take work for nothing.
Say you can't bear it: it won't let you go,

this play of shadows on the screen.

You're tired all day, and at night sleep takes over.
You'll never have time to think of god.
When the god on the hill stands before you,
you'll know: Life is nothing but show,

this play of shadows on the screen.

ACP 220, 3:75
ŏkkaṭi taruvāta ver' ŏkaṭai kācukuṇḍu

Can you cut water in two?
Why hesitate? Take this woman.

The moon may have a dark spot,
but is the moonlight stained?
Her face may show anger,
but there's no anger in her heart.

Can you cut water in two?

Lotus petals may look sharp at the edges,
but their fragrance has no edge.
Sometimes she looks at you sharply,
but the smile in her eyes is always soft.

Can you cut water in two?

All the toughness in the coconut
is on the surface.
There's nothing tough inside.
God on the hill: it's only a mask.
Make love to her. She'll melt and flow.

Can you cut water in two?

SCP 263, 9:44
nīṭi naḍu maḍacite neḍu rĕṇḍ' aunā

Lord, I give up.
There's nothing like you in this world.

I can say I'm not frightened by anything,
but the courage must come from you.
I can boast of my strength, any time,
but inside me, all awareness is you.

I give up.

I can claim to be fully awake,
but you have to give me wisdom.
I'd like to think I'm free from fantasy.
Fantasy comes from you.

I give up.

Suppose I say I've conquered birth.
Only you can make me free.
I'd bring you some gift,
god on the hill,
but you already own the world.

I give up.

ACP 228, 3:107
sarveśvarā nīku śaraṇu cŏccitim' ide

You're too shy to tell him you have your period.
We don't know where this will lead.

You hold your cheeks in your hand and giggle
because your man looks at you.
If he comes to touch you now in *those* places,
what will you do?

We don't know where this will lead.

You cross your legs and bend your head,
thrilled that he calls you to bed.
If he comes close to you, twines hand in hand,
won't you go along?

We don't know where this will lead.

You're bathing with wild pleasure
because the god on the hill has touched you.
Now he makes love to you with passion.
Tell me what happened to the taboo.

We don't know where this will lead.

SCP 260, 9:33
cĕragu māsina suddi cĕppa jālakuṇḍevu

I seek refuge, you grant it.
That's what marks us, nothing more.

If I say anything at all
with my filthy mouth,
does it ever ring true?
I have lust for women inside me.
So what if my doorstep is clean?

I seek refuge.

I could read every book,
but if there's greed in my mind,
will I ever come into my own?
If I scrub my body
with my ego in place,
I'm left wearing the guise.

I seek refuge.

Carrying the burden of life,
I may do many good things,
but can I free myself from the fault
of being born?
God on the hill, you are my king.
Do I want more?

I seek refuge.

ACP 244, 3:169
śaraṇu ne jŏccinadi sari nīvu manniñcedi

Mother, who speaks so sweetly,
has gone to sleep.
She made love to her husband
with all her feminine art.

Now our friend is sleeping
long into the day,
hair scattered on her radiant face.

Endlessly inventive,
she played with him,
stealing his mind
until dawn.

Now, upstairs in her golden room,
she's sleeping, her sari slipped
from her breast.

Eyes glistening,
red in the corners,
she made love to the father
of Love.[1] Now she's exhausted.
She's lying on her side,
pearls on her thighs.

The god on the hill
held her in his arms.
She's sleeping,
a half-open flower.

SCP 54, 6:54
paluku deněla talli pavaḷiñcěnu

1. Vishṇu is the father of Manmatha, god of desire.

You're both inside and outside,
leaving no gap.
You keep searching, inside and out.
You are the wind that breathes.

You are the life of pouring moonlight.
You ripple over the deep black ponds.
Soaked in the fragrance of unfolding jasmine,
you seem like water far away.

You are the wind that breathes.

You hold court in the mango grove.
You drink up honey from the lotus pond.
You are where all coolness rests,
but you rain down heat on us.

You are the wind that breathes.

You live up there, on the hill, like a lord.
You make couples happy, after love.
You tickle women between their breasts.
Don't fan the fires of loneliness.

You are the wind that breathes.

SCP 70, 5:159
vĕlin uṇḍi lon uṇḍi vĕlitigāk' uṇḍi

Where is my wisdom?
Where is my good sense?
Time is lost, like an offering
poured in the dust.

I think I need this thing, or maybe that thing.
I never get beyond such hopes.
I keep on waiting, and time lures me
like a deer behind a bush,

an offering poured in the dust.

There's always this plan, or maybe that one,
and my problems will be over.
I go through trick after trick,
trapped in thoughts and hurt.
Time melts like butter next to fire,

an offering poured in the dust.

I'm sure I'll be happy here, or maybe over there,
so I keep moving from place to place.
I don't even see the god right next to me.
Time goes, like empty talk,

an offering poured in the dust.

ACP 7, 1:31
eḍa sujñānam' eḍa tĕlivi nāku

You think I'm someone special,
but I'm just your woman. Nothing more.

I get excited when we talk—and it's not enough.
I keep staring at you—but it's not enough.
We keep making love—and it's not enough.
How did you make me fall for you?

I'm your woman.

I serve you plenty—but I want more.
I bow to you—but I want more.
I think of you all the time—and I want more.
It's all your doing, not mine.

I'm your woman.

I embrace your feet.
I kiss you.
It's not enough. I want more.
God on the hill: I'm Alamelumanga.
I'm the one you chose.
That's all I know.

I'm your woman.

SCP 420, 12:67
yĕnta asodamo yani yĕñcevu sumī

Patience is policy
for women. Don't confront.
Men are soft.

Stubbornness won't work.
Be a friend.
He'll fall for you by himself.
Don't show your strength.
Just laugh.
That's where your skill really lies.

Patience is policy.

Don't make pronouncements.
Just fall on top of him.
He'll lose himself in you.
He'll be yours.
Don't take him to court.
Show some desire.
You can bet it will work.

Patience is policy.

You don't have to be tough.
Seduce him.
Let *him* be strong.
He's made love to you.
Don't point out his flaws.
Be loving.
That's your true talent.

Patience is policy.

SCP 142, 7:154
orupe nerupu summī vuvidalaku

Let him be as big as he wants.
He's a man, after all.

If he looks at a woman,
he wants to be friends.
If you turn on your charm,
he'll connect.
If you send a signal,
you're together.
Why does he play hard to get?

He's a man, after all.

If you smile a little, he turns shy.
Then he'll take any chance to touch you
in certain places.
If you give him a time,
he'll come and make love.
I know him.
Why does he brag about his principles?

He's a man, after all.

You have only to stand before him.
He'll try to embrace you.
When he thinks of you, his desire comes to a boil.
See, he's already made love to me.
He held nothing back.

He's a man, after all.

SCP 469, 12:203
aṭṭe tān ĕntavāḍainān āyagāka

You can't embrace it, you can't reject it.
You'll never escape Love's command.

Women's faces are lamps held up in the market.
Their breasts are golden pots on the front porch.
Luscious mouths, shared honey.
We make love to bodies. Make no mark.

Warm curries on the plate, lover's quarrels, displays of pride,
spots of shade in the hot sun, occasional hours of love,

strings you can't break, mysterious smiles,
pain in the midst of goodness, words within words,

oil poured on fire, hopes that never end,
the space inside desire, like drinking butter
when you're thirsty:

finding the god on the hill
is the one good thing that is real.

ACP I, I:I
valaci pai kŏnaga rādu valadani tŏlaga rādu

You have to solve the riddle you've posed.
Can I do it alone?

A bubble is born in a second from the water
and, for a while, looks like a million.
Then it dissolves back into water.
Is it real or contingent?
Tell me what it means.

You have to solve the riddle.

A breeze is blowing in the sky,
sweeping through the world.
Then it merges into space.
Is it illusion or is it truth?
Tell me what it means.

You have to solve the riddle.

Sprouts shoot up from the soil
to form heaps for the farmer.
Then they die back into the earth.
Do they exist, or do they not?
Tell me what it means.

You have to solve the riddle.

ACP 173, 2:242
nīvu vĕṭṭinaṭṭi cikku nīve tĕlupa valĕ

No one can talk back to you.
No one can even look at you.
Is she doing something wrong?

She makes a sign, throws a flower.
She's burning with desire.
When you look at her, very close,
she covers her breasts.
Is this wrong?

No one can talk back to you.

She's filled with love for you.
Her body tingles all over.
Her cheeks are wet,
she bends her head,
sighing at what you do.
Is that wrong?

No one can talk back to you.

Wanting you so much,
she shies away from you.
She plays at making love.
Young god on the hill,
she's right beside you.
So far, is anything wrong?

No one can talk back to you.

SCP 271, 9:70
āḍarāni cūḍarāni yaṭṭi dŏrav' inte kāka

It's no small thing, this load you carry from the past.
It catches up with you.

You bind everyone in the world in the round of life and death.
For this sin, someone has bound that woman
to your chest,[2] not sparing you even though
you're god.

It catches up with you.

Just for fun, you drown living beings
in the ocean of life, and then you dredge them up.
For this flaw, they make you sleep
on the ocean, even if
you're god.

It catches up with you.

You drive us through forests and over mountains.
You never let us rest.
That's why you have to live up on that hill
as the Lord of the Lake,[3] whether you like it
or not.

It catches up with you.

ACP 32, 1:133
sāmānyamā pūrvasaṅgrahamb' agu phalamu

2. Lakṣmī/Śrī, Vishṇu's wife, is said to dwell on his chest.

3. Veṅkaṭeśvara's shrine is on the banks of the Svāmi-puṣkariṇī tank (*koneru*).

He's the master. What can I say
when he says I'm better than the others?

I don't even have to ask.
He takes whatever I say as a command.
Why should I brag?
My husband is under my thumb.

He's the master.

Who am I to serve him, when *he*
takes joy in serving me?
How can I tell you the thousand ways
he's with me?
He knows everything, just like god,
and *he* praises me.

He's the master.

I'm always in his arms.
He's always laughing with me.
He's the god on the hill
and I'm Alamelumanga.
Do I have to make a statement?
He's my slave.

He's the master.

SCP 419, 12:65
yėlinavāḍu tānu yem' anagala nenu

Imagine that I wasn't here. What would you do with your kindness?
You get a good name because of me.

I'm number one among idiots. A huge mountain of ego.
Rich in weakness, in giving in to my senses.
You're lucky you found me. Try not to lose me.

Imagine that I wasn't here.

I'm the Emperor of Confusion, of life and death.
Listed in the book of bad karma.
I wallow in births, womb after womb.
Even if you try, could you find another like me?

Imagine that I wasn't here.

Think it over. By saving someone so low,
you win praise all over the world.
You get merit from me, and I get life
out of you. We're right for each other,
god on the hill.

Imagine that I wasn't here.

ACP 208, 3:33
nen' ŏkkaḍa lekuṇḍite nī kṛpaku pātram' edi

This is the magic love works on men and women.
Whatever they do ends in joy.

Even when their anger goes far,
it's still beautiful.
A man won't rebuff his woman.
Even if you raise an eyebrow,
he won't be upset.

It ends in joy.

You can touch over and over.
The body doesn't tire.
No matter how often you make love,
you're never sated.

It ends in joy.

If he keeps asking for more,
it does no harm.
He's god.
I'm his wife.
We've had this happiness
since we were young.

It ends in joy.

SCP 427, 12:93
maruḍu sesina māya

She heard that only silent sages see him.
She won't talk to anyone anymore.

He loves people who fast for him.
So she was told.
Since yesterday she's stopped eating.
She learned that people who pray in the woods
are his closest friends.
Now she won't leave the garden.

Thinking about god is best of all,
so she sits there with her face in her hands.
They said he's master of the gods,
so just like them, day and night,
she never blinks.

They told her you can find him in water,
so she no longer wipes away her sweat.
This good god is the god of the hills.
She presses against him
with her breasts.

SCP 2, 5:5
tagilina munule yātani gandur' aṇṭā

Those priceless cowgirls are more fun.
Why would you want women
who come to you on their own?

Eyes flashing, words aflame,
we take bets that we can excite you.
We laugh, we tease, we touch,
and we're always there for you.
Why love *us?*

Those cowgirls are more fun.

We banter, we give betel,
we provoke you.
We give you gifts,
we always want you.
Why treat *us* as your friends?

Those cowgirls are more fun.

Even with our eyes, we bow to you.
We wait, we hope,
we follow your signs.
Why should you like *us?*
God on the hill, you've made love to us.
Will anyone else want you more?

Those cowgirls are more fun.

SCP 432, 12:107
vĕlaleni gŏllĕtale veḍuka gāka

You keep asking me all these questions, but I've forgotten.
You're god: you know the answers.
Out of love, you gave me birth,
but desire plays its games.

Just try and measure all the milk I've drunk
in birth after birth, from breast after breast.
How many mothers and fathers have been mine?
In what distant lands were they born?
Your accountant knows how many long years I've lived on earth,
and what vast granaries I've consumed.

You're god. You know the answers.

How much cotton have I worn out in all the clothes I have worn?
How much gold have I rubbed away in ornaments on my skin?
Do *you* remember the names of all the women I've slept with?
Only my karma knows what made me live out these days.

You're god. You know the answers.

Many are the places where I built houses and owned land.
So much pain: what was it all for? Why have I lived so long?
You're inside everyone. You're the reason.
You're endlessly kind, god on the hill. Now it's up to you.

You're god. You know the answers.

ACP 143, 2:127
anniyun aḍugave nene maracitin

You may be god, but
don't blame us.

The world you created has many faces
and is in itself unstable.
With all your miracles, even you can't leave it.
And we who live here—how can we let go?

Don't blame us.

Nature plays many games,
takes in all our senses.
You yourself live there.
Can ordinary people give it up?

Don't blame us.

You're the only one, Lord,
who could turn off your illusion.
No one else can do it.
All we can do is surrender.

Don't blame us.

ACP 179, 2:267
jalajanābha hari jaya jaya

You tell him about subtlety.
If I insist, they'll say I'm too demanding.

Instead of talking back to me,
he would do better to send a messenger.
Why stare at me over and over?
He might bend his head, a little shy.

Tell him about subtlety.

Better than laughing so loudly,
he could be a little quiet.
Instead of pestering me to play,
let him simmer with some affection.

Tell him about subtlety.

Rather than tiring me by making love,
let him lie quietly by my side.
I'm Alamelumanga. He's the god on the hill.
A loving touch would make all the difference.

Tell him about subtlety.

SCP 419, 12:63
yĕrigiñcare patiki yī suddul ĕllānu

Are you the same crazy kid
who stole the butter?
You can't be seen or heard.

You hold in your belly
all those people who don't accept you.
When the dying man said nāra,
asking for coconut fibers,
you heard it as your name, Nārāyaṇa,
and saved him, like a hero.

Are you crazy?

You become a slave to your servants.
You run after them.
Craving a mere handful of rice,[4]
you made yourself ridiculous.

Are you crazy?

You've taken thousands of names
so that people can choose what name they want.
Now you're the god on the hill.
Easy to reach.

Are you crazy?

ACP 106, 2:22
vĕnnalu dŏṅgilunāṭi vĕrrivā nīvu

4. Krishna yearned for the poor man Sudāma's gift of a handful of pounded rice; in exchange, he made Sudāma wealthy.

Lord, it's up to you
to discipline my mind.
You live in me.

It's like an elephant out of control.
It goes crazy again and again.
It's like mercury, never contained,
always slipping away.

You live in me.

It's like a deer in the wilderness.
The more you try to catch it,
the more it runs away.
It's like a wild wind at play.

You live in me.

Like the ocean, it takes in everything.
You have to look after it, god on the hill.
Tell it to come to you.

You live in me.

ACP 179, 2:266
hari nīve buddhi cĕppi

These marks of black musk
on her lips, red as buds,
what are they but letters of love
sent by our friend to her lover?

Her eyes the eyes of a *cakora* bird,
why are they red in the corners?

Think it over, my friends:
what is it but the blood
still staining the long glances
that pierced her beloved
after she drew them from his body
back to her eyes?

What are they but letters of love?

How is it that this woman's breasts
show so bright through her sari?

Can't you guess, my friends?
It's the rays from the crescents
left by the nails of her lover,
rays luminous as moonlight on a summer night?

What are they but letters of love?

What are these graces,
these pearls,
raining down her cheeks?

Can't you imagine, friends?
What could they be but beads of sweat
left on her gentle face
by the god on the hill
when he pressed hard,
frantic in love?

What are they but letters of love?

SCP 14, 5:57
emŏkŏ ciguruṭadharamuna

You're just about as much as one imagines you to be.
As they say, the more dough, the more bread.

People who follow Vishṇu love you as Vishṇu.
Philosophers speak of you as the ultimate.
Those who go with Śiva think of you as Śiva.
Those who carry skulls see a skull in your hand.[5]

You are as one imagines.

People who serve the goddess think you are their goddess.
Different schools of thought measure you by their thoughts.
Small people think of you to get rich, and for them you become small.
Thoughtful minds contemplate your depths, and for them you are deep,

as deep as one imagines.

There's nothing missing in you.
The lotus spreads to the limits of the lake.
There's water in the Ganges, also in wells on the shore.
You're the god on the hill,
the one who's taken hold of me.
For me, you are real,

as real as I imagine.

ACP 179, 2:265
ĕnta mātramunan ĕvvaru talacina

5. Bhairava, the form of Śiva worshiped by the Kāpālikas, carries a skull.

Bring a lamp where it's dark.
Why bring light to light?

Why take care of whoever is happy?
Shelter those in distress.
You really should rescue the drowning.
Who needs *you* to save the man on the shore?

Why bring light to light?

Why worry about those who are free?
Release the ones trapped in themselves.
You really should feed the famished.
Who needs *you* to fill those who are full?

Why bring light to light?

You should stand by the man of a million sins,
not by those who always do good.
If you won't help the weak,
god on the hill,
who needs *you*?

Why bring light to light?

ACP 3, 1:12
tĕliya cīkaṭiki dīpam' ĕttaka

Better keep your distance
than love and part—
especially if you can't manage
seizures of passion.

Make love, get close, ask for more—
but it's hard to separate and burn.
Open your eyes to desire,
then you can't bear to shut it out.

Better keep your distance.

The first tight embrace is easy,
but later you can never let go.
Begin your love talk—
once hooked, you can never forget.

Better keep your distance.

Twining and joining, you can laugh.
Soon you can't hide the love in your heart.
Once the god on the hill has made love to you,
you can no longer say
it was this much and that much.

Better keep your distance.

SCP 484, 12:252
tagili pāyuṭa kaṇṭe

Born a man.
Serves another man.
Suffers every day.

Goes into every wretched place
and begs for a morsel to eat.
Craves the place he was born.
That's why he's never free.

Born a man.

God is born in all of us.
Grows in all of us.
Is all of us.
If a man chooses him,
he goes where no one else can go.

Born a man.

ACP 32, 1:131
manujuḍai puṭṭi manujuni seviñci

You're not easy to reach, but somehow
you're available. The more I think about it,
the more I'm surprised.

One has to read so many books
and ask so many people
just to know how to know you.
How many good things must one do
even to begin to want you!

You're not easy to reach.

I have to go through many births,
search many places,
before I see you with my eyes.
I have to wait a long time in line
before I get a chance to serve you.

You're not easy to reach.

I have to learn so much
and practice over and over
before you know me as your man.
You have done it *for* me.
I don't even have the words.

You're not easy to reach.

ACP 164, 2:208
iṭṭivāḍavu sulabham' ĕṭlān aitivo kāka

How can I conquer my senses?
They're too strong.

Our eyes, small as a grain of sand,
reach all the way up to the sky.
Our tiny ears
touch the music beyond.

They're too strong.

This nose, no bigger
than a sesame seed,
captures the wind.
Lying in wait in the mouth,
this stub of a tongue
eats everything.

They're too strong.

Pleasures of the body's surface
yield the whole world.
When the mind knows the god on the hill
through and through,
the body reaches the shore.

They're too strong.

ACP 208, 3:32
ĕṭṭu gĕlutu pañcendriyamula

What can I say about my crazy ways?
Just laugh them off.
Take care of me.

You speak through me,
and I'm proud of my eloquence.
You control the whole world,
but I think I'm the king.

What can I say?

You create all these people,
and then I think *I'm* my children's father.
You give whatever I have,
but I'm sure I've earned it all.

What can I say?

You give this world and the other,
and I think I've won them by my prayers.
You're not finished with me yet.
I'm the great expert
on God.

What can I say?

ACP 163, 2:203
iṭṭi nā vĕrritanamul em' ani cĕppu kŏndunu

Don't you know my house,
the palace of the love god,
flooded with the sweet smell of flowers?

Don't you know the house
in the shade of the tamarind grove,
that narrow space between golden hills?

That's where you lose your senses,
where the love god hunts without fear.

Don't you know my house?

Don't you know the house,
the love god's marketplace,
where the dark clears and yet does not clear?

Don't you know the house
where you live in your own heart?
That's where feelings hold court.

Don't you know my house?

Don't you know the house
in the crazy garden?[6]
You should know. You're the god on the hill.

Its gates are sealed by the love god.
That's where you heap
all your wealth.

Don't you know my house?

SCP 75, 5:179
maruninagari daṇḍa mā yill' ĕragavā

6. Literally, the garden of the *ummĕtta,* a fruit that, if eaten, is supposed to drive one insane.

I'm so happy I chose to marry you.
You're a big man now.
What can I say?

You're a skilled lover, and you're only
one man. But your affairs
are counted by the million.
If I look at your bed, I see sixteen thousand women.
I can't know your mystery.
What can I say?

If you really want to, you can put a woman on your chest[7]
or ask her to sit on your head.
If I open your door, there are cow-girls all over.
I can't win.
What can I say?

If you lie down, you're Govindarāja.[8]
If you stand up, you're the god on the hill.
Two women are always at your feet.
Among all of them, you cared for me.
What can I say?

SCP 1356, 23:222
santosiñcitimi ninnu callagā bĕṇḍlāḍitini

7. Lakṣmī dwells on Vishṇu's breast.
8. Govindarāja in Tirupati is in a reclining posture.

There's nothing you don't know.
I do what you say.
I'm your man.
Where am I in all this?

You made eyes for seeing,
so why blame me when I look?
You made ears for beautiful sounds.
I act, but you've set me up.

Where am I in all this?

If it tastes good, I chew it.
It's only natural.
I didn't make up the rules.
If it smells good, the nose smells it.
Why tie me in knots?

Where am I in all this?

It's the nature of one body
to melt into another.
Why tell me I'm doing something wrong?
You've snared me, god on the hill,
but you're always inside me.
Who is to blame?

Where am I in all this?

ACP 180, 2:268
nīv' ĕraganidi ledu nīy ājña mocitin' inte

Why step in the mud and then wash your feet?
Why swim through the oceans of birth?

You do many bad things
because you're in love with yourself.
Self-love is fed by false hope.
Hope feeds on desire.
Attachment is the root of all this.

Why step in the mud?

Endless attachment leads to grief.
Grief is a fire in the heart.
Fire can burn you to death.
Your mind is the root of all this.

Why step in the mud?

The god on the hill made your mind.
Only you can make it think of him.
The thoughts in your mind are partly god
and partly you.
Think him through.

Why step in the mud?

ACP 41, 1:168
kaḍun aḍusu coran ela kāḷḷu gaḍugagan ela

Pour milk on the bitter neem.
Will that make it sweet?

Stretch a dog's tail,
flatten it with sticks—
will it ever become straight?
Train your body over and over.
Will it ever behave?

Pour milk on the bitter neem.

Soak an ax in water as long as you want.
Will it ever be soft?
The mind addicted to wrong ways—
however long you beat it,
will it ever bend?

Pour milk on the bitter neem.

You can shelter a scorpion in your pocket,
but don't be surprised if it stings.
Desire goes on forever.
Will it ever end?

Pour milk on the bitter neem.

ACP 47, 1:192
bhāramaina vepamānu pālu vosi pĕñcinānu

To say "Let's make love" is more beautiful
than making love.
Pangs of longing are deeper than fulfillment.

Better than being close
is the pain of wanting you from afar,
the mad dream of making love.
Sweeter than hugging you, warm in bed,
is stealing a look from the edge of my eye.

Say "Let's make love."

More to my liking than having fun
are the sharp words of our quarrels.
The flowers you throw at me give me more
than your soothing touch when I reach for you.

Say "Let's make love."

Happier than sleep after giving in to passion
is one long, tight embrace.
God on the hill, you made love to me.
Doing it is better than saving your pride.

Say "Let's make love."

SCP 1633, 26:137
kūḍi sukhiñcuṭa kaṇṭĕ kūḍudam' anede impu

How can we describe the feeling she has for you?
It's like spring bursting all over.

There's no room in her thoughts
to hide her shy hopes.
They're spilling out as smiles,
past the corners of her lips.
No way to hold her love inside—
it keeps bubbling out in words.

How can we describe it?

She has no place to stash away
her boundless dreams.
They gleam through glances
from the corners of her eyes.
Her desire is everywhere. She can't suppress it.
It's flowing from all her pores.

How can we describe it?

She can't contain the joy of making love.
It's emerging as light on her face.
You've touched her,
god on the hill.
Now she plays with you.

How can we describe it?

SCP 491, 12:278
yem' ani vinnaviñcemu

We're all alike: that's what the Veda says.
God treats us all the same.

The ant thinks it's happy as an ant.
A mosquito is happy as itself.
A fly in spring feels happy all its life.
Is one happier than the next?

We're all alike.

We're all born, we all die.
We eat, sleep, and couple.
Does anyone have more than this?

We're all alike.

Whoever we may be,
to think of the god on the hill
is solace.
Wherever you look, he's inside.
No one can move
without him.

We're all alike.

ACP 182, 2:276
samabuddhey indariki sarvavedasāramu

I'm trying to be patient,
but you don't know who I am.
You're showing off in front of me.

Just dressing up won't give you class.
Big breasts don't make you a good lover.
Fine clothes can't make you a queen.
And you want to talk to my man!

I'm trying to be patient.

Tie your hair in a high bun: it won't help.
Will chewing betel make you a connoisseur?
You can rest your palm on your cheek all you want.
Will it bring men to your lap?
And you want to laugh with my man!

I'm trying to be patient.

Sitting next to him doesn't make you his friend.
You can touch body to body. It still gives you no grace.
The god on the hill has a wife, true,
but he's attuned to *my* feeling.
He's made love to me.
What are you going to do about it?

I'm trying to be patient.

SCP 1317, 23:67
ĕnta vorucukuṇḍinān ĕragavu nā mundara

Is there some way I can reach you?
You have no end and no beginning.

I want to praise your good qualities,
but you have no qualities.
I try to think of you in my mind.
You sit behind every thought.

Is there some way I can reach you?

I want to worship you with my hands,
but you are huge, you fill all space.
I would bring you a gift, but you have everything
in the world.

Is there some way I can reach you?

I want to see you with my eyes.
You have no visible form.
God on the hill, you're in all these things.
All I can say is, I am yours.

Is there some way I can reach you?

ACP 131, 2:82
ed' upāyamu ye ninnu teruṭaku

I can't tell what lies ahead, what lies behind.
I must be crazy.
Is there a cure for the cravings of my mind?

I pray that I'll get rich in my future lives,
but in what body will I be born?
I make my bed, I go to sleep
without wondering if I'll wake up.

Is there a cure?

When dawn breaks, I tell myself I'm awake.
Is it a lie, or is it true? Do I know?
I have a way of making women want me.
I don't see my body getting old.

Is there a cure?

I do bad things, I forget, I go on.
The accountant is keeping tabs.
I've looked for god in some distant places.
I didn't know he's right beside me.

Is there a cure?

ACP 103, 2:11
vĕnak' edo mundar' edo vĕrri nenu

He's worn out. Bring him to me.
I'm the specialist in that disease.

Too many eyes have pierced him.
I may have to use love-charms, extra-strength.
His muscles are sore from battling breasts.
I'll massage him with a warm embrace.

I'm the specialist.

He must be exhausted from so much loving.
I'll touch him with the herb that revives.
His sensitive parts have melted down.
I'll bring them to life
with charms of shyness.

I'm the specialist.

Those artless women—how exciting can they be?
I have the right drug.
He's the handsome god on the hill,
and I'm Alamelumanga.
He's with me now. I can cure him.

I'm the specialist.

SCP 469, 12:202
tān ela vasivāḍī daggara rammanave

What can I say about other women?
A loving wife thinks only of you.

Even if you don't make love to her,
she looks at you and laughs for you.
She's the best.
Even if you don't call her, she comes on her own
to be with you.
She's the best.

You can forget all about her,
but she'll still come and excite you.
She loves you. She's really the best.
Your thoughts are elsewhere,
you don't even notice her,
so she stands before you and makes you look.
She's the best.

Even if you make love to other women
once in a while,
she takes pleasure in it.
She's wholly good.
You've taken Alamelumanga,
god on the hill,
and made her happy.
You can't leave her.
She's the best.

SCP 433, 12:113
yitara satula mariy emi cĕppedi

What profit will you get
out of hiding from me?
I'm right here, and I want you.

Those fantastic eyes—do you want to lock them in a bank?
You don't even raise your head to look at me.
Do you think you can invest that amazing smile at a good rate?
I can't get you to smile at me.

What profit will you get?

Those towering breasts—are you going to put them in a vault?
You're hiding them under your sari.
Are you planning to hoard underground
the full bloom of your youth?
You keep so still under your veil.

What profit will you get?

You want to stash away words instead of spending them in love?
You don't even move your lips.
You belong to me now, and I—
I'm God.
At last we can do business.

What profit will you get?

SCP 471, 12:207
inta guṭṭu sesukōniy emi gaṭṭu kōneve

I may never know you,
but you are my lord.
Come to me. No more games.

I really can't stop wanting you,
so I get angry and turn to sarcasm.
Over and over, I dream of making love.
It doesn't happen. I get upset.

Come to me.

Irritated that I can't see you,
I find fault with everything.
I want you to want me on your own.
I shake my fists at shadows.
I'm so tired.

Come to me.

No one can measure your love.
Embracing you, I am proud.
You've taken me to the limit
of loving, god on the hill.
I've taken you in. This is joy.

Come to me.

SCP 430, 12:103
yĕnta nen ĕragakunnān eppuḍū nīve gati

We're happy when you're together.
We can't stand it when you're at odds.

Your eyes are separate, but the look is the same.
You're not talking to one another,
but between you, you're one person.
You sit there, forlorn. She's here, hands on her cheeks.
It's too much for us to bear

when you're at odds.

Your ears may be separate, but what you hear is the same.
Your passion for each other is one.
Now she's on the bed, you're on the porch.
We can't force you to make up

when you're at odds.

Your arms may be separate, your embrace is the same.
When you make love, you are one.
When the two of you quarrel, god on the hill,
can we take sides

when you're at odds?

SCP 261, 9:38
kadisina mimu mĕcca galamu gākā

All connections
are with god.
If you know this,
you won't get stuck.

The moment you look, you get attached.
If you start talking, you make it worse.
If you smile, you're deeper in it.
Turn away, you won't be caught.

All connections are with god.

If you open your ears, the whole world grabs you.
Live in the world, and you're trapped.
The more you live, the more you are bound.
Turn away, say nothing, you won't be caught.

All connections are with god.

You want to help, you want to give:
you only tighten your chains.
If you want control,
you are totally lost.
Set your mind on god alone, and
nothing binds you.

All connections are with god.

ACP 145, 2:137
daivamutoḍide tana tagulu

Talk to her. Why turn your face away?
Here is a gift from her to you.

How long can a woman in love
stay away from you?
How long can pride last?
The bride always loses in pouring the rice.[9]
She's not your rival. Take the gift.

Talk to her.

How can a woman stay stubborn
when she's sharing your bed?
Once she belongs to you,
how long can she quarrel?
A woman's heart is like butter.
How hard can it be?
Don't forget the secret touch.
Take the gift.

Talk to her.

How tough can she be
when she wants you right now?
She's suffering from separation.
How separate can she be?
You took her, god on the hill.
You loved her. Now she's happy.
Take the gift.

Talk to her.

SCP 435, 12:119
avvali mom' el' ayyev' āpĕto māṭāḍavayya

9. At the wedding, bride and groom are given yellow rice to pour on each other's head. Whoever pours more quickly wins, but the bride always loses.

If even people in high places
have to suffer their karma,
what about people like me?

Once you killed that snake.[10]
Now you have to sleep on a big snake.[11]
Ever since you killed that woman,[12]
you bear another one on your chest.[13]

What about people like me?

Because you broke a cart,[14]
you had to go to work as a driver.[15]
Once you uprooted a mountain.[16]
Now you're stuck up on the hill.

What about people like me?

ACP 45, I:185
ěṭṭivārikin ěllan iṭṭi karmamulu

10. Kāliya, on whose head Krishna danced.
11. Vishṇu sleeps on the thousand-headed serpent Ādiśeṣa.
12. Tātakā, slain by Rāma.
13. Lakshmī/Śrī, who lives on Vishṇu's breast.
14. Śakaṭâsura, the cart-demon killed by Krishna.
15. Krishna was Arjuna's chariot driver in the *Mahābhārata* battle.
16. Govardhana, lifted by Krishna to shelter the cowherds of Braj.

She's a woman, after all.
Cut it out.
Her sari is soaked with sweat.

She's trying to do up her hair.
You peek under her arms and smile,
so she brings her arms down
out of shyness, and her hair
is all over her face.

Cut it out.

She's trying to put on her sari.
You sneak a look at her thighs and smile,
so she sits down in confusion,
her belt snaps, the sari falls in a heap.

Cut it out.

She's putting on her necklace.
You catch a glimpse of her breasts and smile.
She hugs you to hide herself,
and her body breaks out in goosebumps.

Cut it out.

SCP 3078, 23:313
āḍuvāri nīv' inta āgaḍālu setu ra

You lie hidden both inside and out.
That's why we can't see who you are.

You give the illusion
that you fill all things,
but you are not any one thing.
The echo we hear in the hills
is not a hill, nor is it *in* the hills.

They say you move through everything,
but you are not in any thing.
We see many images in the mirror.
None of them is *in* the mirror.

It's not that you're present in everything,
but neither are you absent from anything.
You are the light that never goes out.
Complete from head to foot.

ACP 44, 1:181
nī mahattvambu loniki vĕlupaliki gappi

If you want another love,
how about a little privacy?
Why open up one woman
to another?

With your head on *her* thigh,
you smile at me.
As *she* is combing your hair,
you tug at the edge of my sari.
What can I say about your tricks?

How about a little privacy?

You put your hand on *her* shoulder,
but you look straight at me.
She hugs you to *her* breasts,
while you press your foot to mine.
Is that how you play?

How about a little privacy?

Reckless, you make love to *her*
while you fold me in your blanket.
When you're done with her, god on the hill,
you turn to me. Only you
can get away with it.

How about a little privacy?

SCP 490, 12:275
valapu pai kŏsaraite vaḍi mogacāṭu gādā

The loveliness of this woman
can't be measured.
Think about it, my friends.

Her long black hair flows like night.
Her face is brilliant as the sun.
Night and day have lined up
front to back.

Think about it.

Her breasts so high,
her waist thin as empty space—
hills and sky
are upside down.

Think about it.

Her hands hold the shoulders
of the god on the hill
and his hands cover her breasts:
branch and vines
intertwined.

Think about it.

SCP 496, 12:294
kŏmma siṅgāramul' ivi kŏladi vĕṭṭaga rāvu

Why learn more? Why read books?
The mind never learns to rest.

An ignoramus reads and reads,
and his greed is compounded with interest.
When a blind dog goes to the market,
what it gets is the stick.

Why learn more?

If you go around blaming god,
you'll never know his mind.
If you don't give yourself
to the god on the hill,
your mind will never be free.

Why learn more?

ACP 32, 1:132
tanak' eḍa caduvulu

Tell her he's standing right next to her,
and he's amazed she doesn't see him.

She's thinking so much, and missing him,
that when he comes to her door and calls her,
she doesn't hear.
Right from the beginning, this separation
has worn her down.
Now if anyone tells her the truth,
she doesn't believe him.

He's standing right next to her.

Drowning in sighs, her hair unkempt,
she doesn't know him even when he touches her.
She's been waiting too long. She's so tired.
When he comes for real, she says it's a lie.

He's standing right next to her.

She lies on a bed of flowers,
her sari slipping from her breasts.
He lies down beside her, she doesn't see him.
Then he looks up and makes love to her,
and she says she's had the strangest dream.

He's standing right next to her.

SCP 275, 9:86
ŏyyanĕ vinnaviñcare vŏddanunna pati jūpi

You don't have to get rid of it.
You don't have to hold on to it.
All you have to do is to be you.
All knots will be untied.

If you have god in your thoughts every day,
you'll forget what worries you.
Like a lemon you're clutching
when you fall asleep,
karma will fall away.
You'll be free.

You don't have to get rid of it.

Serve your master, and the mist will clear.
You'll know yourself more and more.
When you wake up, you see it was a dream.
The life that holds you is only a thought.

You don't have to get rid of it.

When you begin to see god next to you,
you'll hold earth and heaven
in your hand. You'll change.
There's a stone that turns iron to gold.
The dross will fall away.

You don't have to get rid of it.

ACP 370, 4:278
nenai viḍuva vaddu tānai tagula vaddu

What love? What friendship?
They're only words.
Nothing lasts.

Lightning flashes.
Does it linger in the monsoon sky?
A woman's love engulfs you.
Is it forever?

What love? What friendship?

Mirages flow like rivers.
Can they quench your thirst?
A woman's heart seems full of love.
Can it give you strength?

What love? What friendship?

You see gold in your dream.
Does it still glitter when you wake?
Beautiful women are a false hope.
Do they make you think of god?

What love? What friendship?

ACP 36, 1:147
eḍa valap' eḍa maccik' eḍa suddulu

You needn't come any closer.
Just ask me from a distance.
Did I ever say no to you?

Don't stand beside me and beg.
The flowers in my hair might fall on you.
You don't have to squeeze my hands.
The stones in my rings might hurt you.

You needn't come any closer.

Don't take me on your lap and stroke me.
The musk I dabbed on my ears might stain you.
You don't have to hold me to make me say yes.
You might be scorched by my sighs.

You needn't come any closer.

You embrace me, you coax me:
you'll have sandal all over you,
straight off my breasts.
You made love to me, god on the hill.
Now you're drowning in *my* passion.

You needn't come any closer.

SCP 474, 12:218
allantan uṇḍe māṭal ānatīv' ayya

I know him. He knows you.
Am I standing in your way?
Why be jealous?

He married me. He laughs with me.
Why are you making such a fuss?
You're no match for me.
I'm the one who caught his eye.
I touched him. Did I say anything
about you?

Why be jealous?

He put his hand on me. He's my husband.
He overcame my shyness.
Why put on airs?
You're no match for me.
I sought his friendship.
I did what was right.
Did I block your moves?

Why be jealous?

The god on the hill is all over me.
He's god.
Why be stubborn?
You're no match for me.
I'm Alamelumanga. I'm his wife.
I see what you're up to.

Why be jealous?

SCP 418, 12:61
ātani nen' ĕrugudun' ātaḍu nī voj' ĕrugu

Anyone obsessed with love
would become like him.

He's addicted to both his wives.
That's why he needs four hands.[17]
He's done it thousands of times
in all kinds of ways.
No wonder he has so many forms.

Anyone would become like him.

He especially likes love after quarrels.
That's why at times he turns his face away.
He's handsome beyond compare. Playful, too.
Notice his long fingernails.

Anyone would become like him.

Because he likes pleasure to last forever,
he's come to live on this solid mountain.
Bound to life in this world,
he lives inside everyone.

Anyone would become like him.

ACP 17:105, 1:72
talapu kāmâturatvamu mīdan alavaḍina

17. The icon of Veṅkaṭeśvara has four arms.

We get a lot out of you.
You don't have that skill.
God, your servants are better than you.

We grab you with a show of devotion.
We stick you in our mind.
For a little basil on your feet,
we've got freedom wholesale.
Your servants are very clever.

You don't have that skill.

Giving back what you've created,
we suck up all your goodness.
We've figured it out.
We bow once and twice, and put the burden
on you.

You don't have that skill.

We bring water from the pond, sprinkle a little on you,
and get whatever we ask.
God on the hill, with tricks like these,
we always come out on top.

You don't have that skill.

ACP 209, 3:33
nīve neravu gāni ninnu baṇḍiñcemu nemu

It's always your fault, and you always blame the girl.
When you crush body to body,
I scratch you with my nails.

You put your hand on me when I'm feeling shy.
I draw myself up and yell at you.
You want me when I'm lying down,
covered with a blanket.
I grab a flower and throw it at you.

It's always your fault.

I'm sitting, head bent.
You fondle me and pull at my sari.
I get angry and shake my finger.
I'm spinning in circles, holding to a pillar.[18]
You pick that moment to approach me, I pound you
with my breasts.

It's always your fault.

I'm massaging your feet, you pull me up
and embrace me. I bite your lips
without thinking twice.
God on the hill, you make love to me.
I suppose I should be grateful.

It's always your fault.

SCP 566, 13:198
nī neram' ĕñcukoka nĕlatanu dūrevu

18. Girls play at spinning themselves in circles while singing a rhyme.

If you don't forget what's outside, there is no inside.
If you have the outside in you, you forget the inside.
If you keep at it, hour by hour, you'll find joy.

When you see only the light outside, you miss the dark inside.
A man of the world has no knowledge of himself.
If you keep staring at the darkness, the outside turns into light.
Look steadily inside, and you'll see god,

if you don't forget.

Just as sleep eludes you when you keep vigil, on and on,
if you keep spinning in the senses, your mind knows no rest.
If you sleep inside yourself, you won't know the world outside.
Forget—forget your mind—and in the solitude you'll see god,

if you don't forget.

Your sighs, from the space inside, merge with the space outside:
birth and death take place only there.
The breath of god inside is the only link with the space outside.
Steady the winds, going in and out, in the self, and you'll see god,

if you don't forget.

ACP 134, 2:92
vĕlupala maravaka lopala ledu

We can't know where we belong.
Still, we come to Vishnu.

If you have knowledge,
the curtain is wide open.
If you forget, it's closed.
Karma catches you like a noose.
It comes off if you pull it.
They entice us, the games he plays.

Where do we belong?

Heaven is waiting for you, if you're rich in goodness.
Hell lies on the way, rooted in evil.
If you just touch them, they catch you.
The skill is in crossing over.
They entice us, the games he plays.

Where do we belong?

If you are determined, god shows himself.
If you get entangled, he tightens the noose.
If the god on the hill won't take care of us,
they'll entice us, the games he plays.

Where do we belong?

ACP 381, 4:319
ĕndalivāramo nemu yĕraga vasamu gādu

Whose friend are you? Nobody knows.
Every one of us thinks you are hers.

Many women see you before them.
You're what each of them wants you to be.
If one looks for you inside the mind,
you're there, too—just within reach.

Whose friend are you?

Women, with you in their heart, call out
only to you. You answer each one alone.
With tapering fingernails,
they fold their hands before you.
You're the fruit of every prayer.

Whose friend are you?

If we kiss your lips while making love,
you're a feast of many years.
When we dance with you, god on the hill,
each of us holds you in her arms.

Whose friend are you?

SCP 434, 12:117
yĕvvarivāḍavau tān ĕrugarād' ĕvvarike

For anyone else it would be wrong.
In your case, it was right.

You're god. Whatever you choose
is the way.
Whatever you stand for is truth.
When a son fought with his father
over these questions,
you supported the son.
Prahlada is proof.[19]

In your case, it was right.

You're god. If you let it happen,
it's fair.
Whatever you say yes to
is proper.
When a younger brother attacked
his older brother, you supported
the younger. Sugriva is proof.[20]

In your case, it was right.

God on the hill, whatever you do
passes for correct.
Whatever you bring about
is good sense.
You stood beside the grandson
who went to kill his grandfather.
Arjuna is proof.[21]

In your case, it was right.

ACP 165, 2:212
parulak' aiten ide pāpamu gādā

19. Prahlāda, devoted to Vishṇu, argued with his father, the demon Hiraṇya-kaśipu, who denied the existence of this god. Vishṇu then came down as the Man-Lion and killed the father.

20. Rāma helped Sugrīva, king of the monkeys, in his fight with Valin, his older brother.

21. In the *Mahābhārata,* Arjuna engineered the death of the family patriarch, Bhīṣma.

Those who know,
know.
Those who do not,
cannot.

The one in the beginning
is also at the end.
He is what we call god.
What you see before you
is everywhere.
That's what we call the world.

Those who know, know.

What does not perish
will never perish.
To know this is knowledge.
What can die
will die.
It goes round and round.
It's life and death.

Those who know, know.

What went on in the beginning
is still going on.
This is what god makes.
What you don't see now
you didn't seen even then.
The theories *we* make
are a fog.

Those who know, know.

ACP 194, 2:324
ĕruguvār' ĕruguduru

I was better off then.
Better off in my past lives
than in this misery.

When I was born as a worm,
at home in the mud,
I never had these worries.
It's much worse to be human.
I was better off then.

Born as a lowly beast,
subject to so much pain,
I didn't know poverty from riches.
Now I know.
I was better off then.

Committing so many wrongs,
I've fallen into hell.
You were there for me.
I was better off then.

ACP I, I:3
hīna-daśala bōndi itlan uṇḍuta kaṇṭĕ

You don't have to tell me anymore lies.
Whatever you may have done,
did I ever argue with you?

You don't have to convince me.
Don't make promises.
What's eating you?
I never said anything.
Others have a lot to say,
but I never talk,

whatever you may have done.

Don't butter me up.
Cut out these fancy words.
I'm not one to nag you, but
I can't vouch for your family and friends,

whatever you may have done.

I myself will never blame you.
Stop hugging me and kissing.
I never talk back to you.
You made love to me.
I won't ruin your name,

whatever you may have done.

SCP 341, 11:139
pŏddu voka nīvu nāto bŏṅka vaccev' inte kāka

It's not easy to see you.
We're human. You're god.

Thank god for demons.
They pester the gods, and then you want to help,
so you come down to earth, and we get to see you.

It's not easy to see you.

It's even good when goodness fails.
The wise appeal to you, and you come down
to bring goodness back. Then we get a chance
to serve you.

It's not easy to see you.

If you ask us, your devotees
are better than you. You're always with them,
wherever they are, god on the hill.
They tell your stories, and we listen,
over and over, so we have you.

It's not easy to see you.

ACP 138, 2:108
ūrak' aite ninnu gānam' ŏka kāraṇāna gāni

Hey lady. Keep a lid on it.
Stop giggling.

There are lots of married women around, just like you.
They don't tell if he holds their hand.
They keep up the connection and love him
even more. No public announcements.

Keep a lid on it.

Married women keep to the house.
They don't broadcast in the market.
Very quietly they take him
and win his praise.
They don't brag.

Keep a lid on it.

If they're in love, they make love.
They don't show off what they've got.
God on the hill is married to Alamelu.
He's made love to me, too. Nobody thinks
he's *your* husband.

Keep a lid on it.

SCP 1315, 23:61
komaliro intulaku guṭṭu valadā

If I knew nothing, would I serve you?
You showed me your magic: that's why I'm after you.

If you made me an animal, would I think of you?
If you made me a rock, would I look for you?
If you made me a tree, would I praise you?
You made me human. That's why I call you.

You showed me your magic.

If I were an animal, I couldn't bow.
If I were a bird, I couldn't worship.
If I were something else, I couldn't follow you.
You gave me awareness. That's why I blame you.

You showed me your magic.

You made me master of all this and taught me
about the world. Take care of me.
I surrender, god on the hill.
You can't hide from me now that you've

showed me your magic.

ACP 133, 2:91
emin ĕragani nāḍu

To hell with friendship.
To hell with playing games.
Once I believed in them.

To hell with youth.
To hell with good looks.
To hell with vanity.
To hell with power.
To hell with love.
To hell with smiles.
Once I believed in them.

To hell with ego.
To hell with pretense and patience.
To hell with money.
Your time is up.

To hell with riches that make you blind.
To hell with fame.
The god on the hill has noticed me.
I'm rid of all the rest.

ACP 32, 1:130
eṭik' ĕvvari pŏndu yissiro cī cī

What shall I do?

What am I doing?

I'm too stupid to change course.

As for that god,
the lord of the world,
the one who helps everyone,
I'll keep him at a safe distance.
I'm adrift
in an ocean of sins.

That god who saved an elephant,
the ultimate one,
the kind one,
the one on the hill,
I'll never worship *him*.
I love this body
that will die.

ACP 43, 1:177
kiṃ kariṣyāmi kiṃ karomi (Sanskrit padam).
Our thanks to Gary Tubb for insights into the meaning of this poem.

I must be crazy. I dig up a whole mountain
to catch a mouse. God, cure my confusion.

I wander the world, doing all sorts of odd things
for a mouthful of rice.
I live all my life with women
for that one second I forget my body.

I must be crazy.

I build house after house
just to hide myself.
Thoughts flow through my mind
only to help me seem big.

I must be crazy.

I do things without knowing.
My life is a cheap deal.
If I take you, god on the hill, for my god,
what will you say about how I lived?

I must be crazy.

ACP 358, 4:231
ĕnta vĕrri

I can say it under oath.
What I say is true.
You know everything,
and I know nothing.

Sometimes you're easy to find.
Sometimes impossible.
You make me think of you.
You also make me forget you.
You make me say those syllables,
and you make me write them down.
I do nothing
outside of you.

I can say it under oath.

Some days you accept my prayers.
Other days, you don't.
You close my eyes in sleep,
and you wake me up—to you.
You keep me ignorant
but you let me understand you.
You're the one who gave birth to me.
It was none of my doing.

I can say it under oath.

Sometimes you're inside me.
Then you're up on the hill.
You rule over me, indulge me,
help me cross to the other side.
You enslave me to the world—
and then bind me to you.
Time is yours, action all yours.
I'm innocent.

I can say it under oath.

ACP 157, 2:180
satyamu seyaga vaccunu

This woman shows no signs
of missing you, as if you'd never left.
We wonder why.

Thinking of you, seeing you
inside herself, she embraces
open space.[22] Maybe she heard from someone
that space is you.[23]

She shows no signs of missing you.

She sings your praises, sees you take shape
in her words, but she still wants more.
She keeps staring at nothing.
Somewhere she must have heard
that you are everywhere.

She shows no signs of missing you.

Whenever she is with you, in thought or word,
you're there, coupled with her.
They say you're alive in everything.
Now we know what they mean.

She shows no signs of missing you.

SCP 55, 6:61
ninu bāsina yaṭlu nĕlataku viyogadaśal

22. The woman who embraces empty space, under the delusion or hallucination that her absent lover is before her, is a stock figure in Indian poetry.

23. The god is identified with *ākāśa,* the most subtle and pervasive of the elements.

Life day after day is a game.
To find what you cannot see
is truth.

Coming is real. Going is real.
What happens in between is a game.
Right in front of you
lies the endless world.
At the very end
is truth.

We eat food. We wear clothes.
It's all part of this passing game.
The past clings to our body.
When we cross the doorway,
there is truth.

Badness never ends,
and there's never enough good.
In the end, time is a game.
High on the mountain, god is king.
Higher than heaven
is truth.

ACP 299, 3:387
nānāṭi baduku nāṭakamu

I'm no stranger to you.
You're not a borrowed thing.
I won't blame you anymore.
Come home.

I used to stare, my hand on my cheek.
Now that same hand welcomes you with flowers.
I would put my finger on my nose.
Now I like what you do.
Don't ask for promises.
I'm already in love.
I'll give you all my secrets.

Come home.

I was so shy. Now I smile for you.
The same eyes that couldn't hold you
now admire you.
I won't be cross with you anymore.
I'm your girl.
I'm not picky.

Come home.

My lips were parched.
Now they flow with honey.
My hair, once unkempt,
is now decked with flowers.
You're the god on the hill.
I'm Alamelumanga.
You're right for me.

Come home.

SCP 443, 12:145
ne nīku veru gānu nīvu nāk' ĕravu gāvu

So you want to be poets, you idiots?
Try basket weaving.

Who wears flowers that others have used?
No one eats from a leaf someone has soiled.
If you copy the lines I've composed,
they won't be fit for god.

Try basket weaving.

How do you find a single grain
in the bunch of chaff?
Will god reward you for the one good word
in your endless drivel?

Try basket weaving.

You want to collect the betel I spit out,
add a little camphor and chew it again?
You steal my tune to fit your words.
Won't god laugh you out of court?

Try basket weaving.

You pick up the pits I throw away.
You feast on the crumbs I leave over.
Your hollow poetry, it's all fluff.
God has better taste than that.

Try basket weaving.

You sing one good poem and nothing after that—
the one you stole from me.
When you try to weld bronze and dirt,
god treats you like dirt.

Try basket weaving.

A rotten fruit rots from inside.
Stolen poems just don't work.
A thief's mother should lie low.

God doesn't like stolen prayers.
Just bow to him.

Try basket weaving.

A man who eats garlic won't open his mouth.
Mustard seeds slip through the sieve.
You steal and won't answer questions.
Silence will get you nowhere.

Try basket weaving.

No one knows you, not even your neighbors.
You sing through your teeth, you mutter words.
You find fault with others, but you're no good yourself.

Try basket weaving.

Tāllapāka Annamâcāryulu sang for Veṅkaṭeśa.
The world likes his words.
If a certain nobody finds fault,
god doesn't care.

Try basket weaving.

ACP 196, 2:333
vĕrrulāla mīku veḍuka galitenu

These are the prayers I sang at your feet,
the flowers of your fame.
Keep them with you.

Even one poem should be enough
to make you care for me.
Let the rest of them lie in your treasury.
Your name that is endless
is cheap to buy
but worth a lot.
You're my haven,
and you're there for me.
Those poems are all my wealth.

Let them lie in your treasury.

You live on my tongue.
You made me sing to you
in many ways.
You are a god of a thousand names.
Who am I to praise you?
Still, you let me sign *my* name.

Let them lie in your treasury.

I'm not saying this out of pride.
I was celebrating you.
I'm not the author.
I was following you.
Don't look for faults.
You're the god on the hill.

Let them lie in your treasury.

ACP 169, 2:226
dācuko nī pādalaku tagane jesina pūjal'ivi

Afterword

1. *The Poet in the Temple*

First the mountain: a long, serrated ridge dominating the town of Tirupati in southern Andhra Pradesh and extending for miles above the fertile countryside. In the morning, the ridge is a haunting pink-to-gray; by late afternoon it turns purple. At night you can see the lights near the top as well as the illuminated *sopāna-mārga*, stone steps that snake up the middle of the mountain. Wherever you go in Tirupati, at any moment, you are under the spell, the compelling presence, of this mountain where the god Venkaṭeśvara lives.

He has been there a long time. Already in the earliest Tamil poetry, from the early centuries CE, the Venkatam mountain is mentioned as the historic boundary between the area of Tamil speech and the regions to the north. In all likelihood, its god was already there in some form—perhaps, as the medieval mythic tradition suggests, as Varāha, the Boar. Certainly by the time of the long Tamil narrative poem, *Cilappatikāram*, in the middle of the first millenium CE, the god of Veṅkaṭam was Vishṇu, with recognizable iconographic features.[24] Today he stands as a tall black rock with four arms, a golden crown, and rich, bejeweled vestments. Some twenty million pilgrims come to Tirupati each year to see him.

As a result, Tirupati is the wealthiest of all Indian temples, a virtual economic empire ruled by the god through his officers in the Devasthanam, the temple administration. This economic regime has been in place since at least the fifteenth century, as a wealth of epigraphic and other sources attest.[25] The rise of Tirupati from somewhat modest beginnings to the

24. *Cilappatikāram* of Iḷankovaṭikaḷ 11.41–51.

25. See Sanjay Subrahmanyam, "An Eastern El-Dorado: The Tirumala-Tirupati Temple Complex in Early European Views and Ambitions, 1540–1660," in *Syllables of Sky: Studies*

full-fledged political and economic system documented by the medieval inscriptions is a complex story, still not properly understood. There was, we can be sure, an ancient link between the temple and the local and translocal kings of southern Andhra and the northern Tamil country. Local tradition connects this god, Veṅkaṭeśvara, with both the Tŏṇḍaimāns of the northern Coromandel and with the great Choḻa dynasty of the far south (ninth to thirteenth centuries).[26] There is also an enduring memory of a far-reaching transition in both the internal organization and the metaphysics of the Tirupati cult at some point in, roughly, the twelfth century; the name of the philosopher Rāmânuja, systematizer of south Indian Srivaishṇavism—the worship of the god Vishṇu as supreme—is emblematically mentioned in this respect.

One could read the history of this cult as a slow process of transformation, in which the early, rather severe, male-dominated Vaikhānasa vision of the god[27] was driven to expand and incorporate a sensual and personal Pāñcarātra theology, in which the goddess, Śrī or Lakṣmī, plays a central role. Today this goddess exists at Tirupati under the name Padmāvati or Alamelumanga (Tamil: Alar mel mankai), the beloved wife of Veṅkaṭeśvara. But she has no proper place in the shrine at the top of the mountain; instead, she has her own separate temple at Mangapuram, at the foot of the hill. People say Veṅkaṭeśvara walks the fourteen kilometers downhill each night to visit Alamelumanga, and that he then climbs the mountain again before dawn. Hence, each morning he is offered a new set of sandals to make up for the wear and tear that have ruined his previous pair.

Mangapuram is also home to the Tāḷḷapāka family. Beginning in the first half of the fifteenth century, the founder of the Tāḷḷapāka line at Tirupati, the poet we know as Annamayya or Annamâcārya, gave voice to another major historical transition in the character and modes of worship of the Tirupati god. In a sense, Annamayya shows us a Tirupati close to the one

in South Indian Civilization in Honour of Velcheru Narayana Rao, ed. D. Shulman, 338–90 (Delhi: Oxford University Press, 1995); B. Stein, "The Economic Function of a South Indian Temple," *Journal of Asian Studies* 19 (1960): 163–76.

26. Epigraphical evidence attests to a Choḻa presence at Tirupati. See Sadhu Subrahmanyam Sastry, *Report on the Inscriptions of the Devasthanam Collections* (Madras: Sri Mahant's Press, 1930), 104–12.

27. As embodied in Vaikhānasa ritual manuals. See T. Goudriaan, *Kāśyapa's Book of Wisdom (Kāśyapa-jñāna-kāṇḍaḥ): A Ritual Handbook of the Vaikhānasas* (The Hague: Mouton and Company, 1965), and D. Narasimha Reddy, *A Study of Some Minor Temple Festivals According to Pancaratra and Vaikhānasa Agamas* (Tirupati: Padmasri Publications, 1983).

we know today—a highly dynamic and successful entrepreneurial system built around a god of individual, subjective temperament, responsive to each of his visitors. By composing some thirty-two thousand Telugu *padam*-poems to this god (if we are to believe the figure given by his grandson, Cinnanna[28]), Annamayya invented a style of lyrical intimacy that became a form of worship. His surviving poems are also, perhaps, the most accessible and universal achievement of classical Telugu literature, one of the major literatures of premodern India.

Within Telugu literature, Annamayya is something of an island. His name is virtually ignored in the Telugu literary canon that was in place by the early sixteenth century. Similarly, musicologists and musicians generally fail to mention him (until the middle of the twentieth century) as one of their predecessors, despite the vast musical production that he left behind. The medieval grammars of metrics never cite him. Annamayya was a maverick, outside the grand genres and lines of force of Telugu literary ecology. Yet he effectively created and popularized a new genre, the short *padam* song, that spread throughout the Telugu and Tamil regions and later became a major vehicle for Carnatic musical composition.[29]

Before going any farther, we should listen to Annamayya's distinctive voice and take note of his chosen form:

> Where is my wisdom?
> Where is my good sense?
> Time is lost, like an offering
> poured in the dust.
>
> I think I need this thing, or maybe that thing.
> I never get beyond such hopes.
> I keep on waiting, and time lures me
> like a deer behind a bush,
>
> *an offering poured in the dust.*
>
> There's always this plan, or maybe that one,
> and my problems will be over.

28. See below, section 3. Less than half this number of *padams* have survived.

29. See V. Narayana Rao in "Multiple Literary Cultures in Telugu: Court, Temple, and Public," in *Literary Cultures in History*, ed. S Pollock, 408–13 (Berkeley and Los Angeles: University of California Press, 2003).

I go through trick after trick,
trapped in thoughts and hurt.
Time melts like butter next to fire,

an offering poured in the dust.

I'm sure I'll be happy here, or maybe over there,
so I keep moving from place to place.
I don't even see the god right next to me.
Time goes, like empty talk,

an offering poured in the dust.[30]

This song is a *padam* (also *saṇkīrtana*, "poem of praise"): three (rarely two, sometimes four or more) short stanzas *(caraṇam)* preceded by a *pallavi* opening, which also serves as a refrain, tying together each of the stanzas and imparting a certain unity. The *pallavi* often gives the theme, which is then expanded in the *caraṇams*. Each stanza reconnects to the *pallavi* syntactically or semantically or both; thus, in performance, there is a tendency to sing the *pallavi* at the conclusion of each stanza. The final stanza invariably refers directly to Veṅkaṭeśvara, the god on the hill, this reference indicating the approaching end of the song. Repetition of the *pallavi* creates a spiral-like architecture of sound and feeling, ultimately enveloping the listener in an awareness, or an experience, of the god's presence.

Annamayya's songs are normally couched in relatively simple, accessible language, a literary language he invented for this purpose. Deceptively close to everyday speech, this language is, in fact, remarkably resistant to easy interpretation; it is rich with unexpected lexical combinations and subtle nuances of meaning as well as diction specific to this style. Annamayya chooses smooth-flowing, musical syllables, dissolving harsh conjunct consonants if they occur, and generally keeps away from Sanskrit (except for the few *padams* he composed entirely in a particular Sanskrit idiom of his own). Listening to the songs, one has the sense of a voice that is softly but insistently murmuring to us, so intimate as to be almost inside us. At the same time, everything this voice says suggests an intimate knowledge of

30. *Adhyātma* Copper Plate 7, vol. 1:31. Hereafter, *padams* are cited by copper plate number (CP), preceded by A *(adhyātma)* or Ś *(śṛṅgāra)*, and followed by volume and page number in the 1998–99 Devasthanam reprinting of the corpus (29 volumes).

and an easy familiarity with the internal addressee of the poems, the god up on the hill.

In poems like the one we have cited, we also hear or overhear a conversation that is taking place inside the poet's own mind (which may well seem to come from our own mind—these are highly universal texts). He is speaking in the first person, describing an ongoing agony within him—his perpetual restlessness, his attempts at self-deception and rationalization, his frantic sense of futility, his self-proclaimed blindness and self-reproach. He reports, distancing himself slightly, on thoughts or voices that he hears: "I'm sure I'll be happy here, or maybe over there...." There is an acute awareness of the finite nature of time given to human beings and of the poet's utter inability to use this gift that has been lavished, or rather wasted, upon him. What is more, this existential perception is the very condition of the poet's self-awareness. Knowing himself as a single subject, he knows, first, this consistent failure. A confessional quality colors the description, so strong that it obscures the usual distinction between the speaker within the text and the poet who has created "him." In Annamayya's introspective *padams,* these two (male) voices seem to merge. The poem as a whole issues from a place of insight, a point of realization. The god, too, is there at the end, holding out some promise of release from the inner torment.

Such first-person *padams* belong in the category called *adhyātmika,* "metaphysical," by the tradition, basing itself on an editorial division already present in the original copper plates. The term is, however, something of a misnomer. These poems are more introspective than metaphysical; they constitute about one-quarter of the surviving corpus. The rest are classed as *śṛngāra,* "love-poems," and offer detailed, imaginative descriptions of the private love life of the god, Veṅkaṭeśvara, which the poet knows at least as well as the god knows it himself. Very often they are projected onto a feminine persona, as if the god's wife, Alamelumaṅga, or one of his (or her) girlfriends were speaking.

Here is an example:

> When I'm done being angry,
> *then* I'll make love.
> Right now, you should be glad
> I'm listening.
>
> When you flash that big smile,
> I smile back. It doesn't mean I'm not angry.
> You keep looking at me,

so I look, too. It isn't right
to ignore the boss.

Right now you should be glad.

You say something, and I answer.
That doesn't make it a conversation.
You call me to bed, I don't make a fuss.
But unless I want it myself,
it doesn't count as love.

Right now you should be glad.

You hug me, I hug you back.
You can see I'm still burning.
I can't help it, god on the hill,
if I'm engulfed in *your* passion.

Right now you should be glad.[31]

We are overhearing a bedroom conversation conveyed to us by Annamayya. He knows what goes on in that bedroom, and he speaks directly in the woman's voice. She is angry, apparently because of her lover's infidelity. In the course of the poem, however, stanza after stanza, she gradually softens; her protests become progressively weaker until she is swept up by the man's desire and makes love to him—without admitting that she is doing so on her own account. The somewhat biting refrain—"Right now you should be glad"—also undergoes a subtle transformation. When we hear it for the last time, it almost sounds like "Right now I should be glad" (that the quarrel is over, that you are here beside me, embracing me). The evolving direction of the poem and of its imagined vignette is here, as in nearly all the erotic *padams*, one of merging, of emerging harmony; most of these *padams* end with a word expressly indicating lovemaking. But what the listener needs to attend to, above all, is the very delicate flow of nuance and individualized emotional textures. These poems are alive with inner movement and rapidly alternating perspectives, as in any truly subjective space. Each one of them captures a small, unique instant in the always evolving, playful web of relations between the partners. And while certain patterns do recur, in general, *padams* resist stereotypes; each stands alone, complete in itself, with its singular, individualized actors.

Again, the performative dimension is crucial. As one listens to the poem, empathy with the female speaker gradually takes hold. The listener, caught

31. SCP 1617, 26:78.

up in the spiraling repetition and the deepening psychological effect, absorbs a "feminine" mode of a very specific type (regardless of whether this listener is a man or a woman in "real" life)—a mode in which subtle shifts cumulate toward an ultimately harmonious physical and emotional climax. In other words, we live through the same moment-by-moment process that the speaker articulates—so much so that the *padam* is, in the last analysis, not really narrative or descriptive in force but rather generative and effectual, actually creating an internal atmosphere and taking us through a certain sequence. This process may also be said to affect the god who is inside the poem; he, too, enters this feminine domain where he is melted, moved, opened up, made responsive to the women's voices all around him, and made capable of playing freely with these women. On a certain level, the whole point is to work this sort of magic on the god who inhabits the stone and to draw him out of it and closer to us. At the same time, nothing prevents a male listener, including the god, from enjoying these love poems *as a man*, that is, from opening himself up in an imaginative way to the feminine experience so powerfully articulated here in relation to the lively presence of a male lover. In this sense, the love *padams* could be said to expand the listener's sensibility beyond any initial categorical identities, including those implicit in the two genres or modes. We will return to this point.

The editorial division of the corpus into these two classes—*adhyātma* and *śṛṅgāra*—seems to have taken place after the corpus was already complete. Annamayya himself seems not to have been party to this classification. There is reason to believe that it reflects an attempt on the part of the poet's sons to institutionalize and delimit the original, unsettling poetic impulse by applying available terminology in a somewhat rigid manner. The love-poems, in particular, have little in common with the kind of courtly productions usually associated with the word *śṛṅgāra*. Nonetheless, the two modes are, on the whole, relatively distinct. The textbook of *padam* poetics, *Saṅkīrtana-lakṣaṇamu*, composed by Cina Tirumalâcārya two generations after Annamayya, defines *padams* as

> *śrutulai śāstramulai purāṇa-kathalai, sujñānasārambulaiy*
> *atilokâgama-vīthulai vividha-mantrârthambulai nītulai*
> *kṛtulai veṅkaṭa-śaila-vallabha-rati-krīḍā-rahasyambulai*
> *nutulai tāḷulapākayannaya vaco-nūtna-kriyal cĕnn' agun.*[32]

32. *Saṅkīrtana-lakṣaṇamu* 12 in *The Tunes of Divinity: Sankirtana Laksanamu. A Treatise on Hymnody by Tallapaka Cina Tirumalacarya*, ed. Salva Krishnamurthy (Madras: Institute of Asian Studies, 1990).

revealed texts, codes of knowledge, ancient stories, the essence of wisdom, routes to temple rites, embedded with meanings of many *mantras*, guides to the good life, well-made poems, secrets of god Veṅkaṭeśvara's playing at love, prayers to god—such are the new works of Tāḷḷapāka Annamayya.

While the early identifications (with Vedic knowledge, *śāstras, mantras,* and so on) impute certain important qualities to the corpus, it is the long compound *veṅkaṭa-śaila-vallabha-rati-krīḍā-rahasyambulu*—"secrets of god Veṅkaṭeśvara's playing at love"—that energizes the verse. We see at once the prime importance of the so-called *srngara* poems, which reveal these intimate secrets, *rahasya,* of the god's life. In classical Srivaishnavism, drawing its lexicon from as far back as the *Bhagavad-gīta* (11.2, 18.68), metaphysical knowledge is always the true secret, *guhya* or *rahasya,* available only to initiates. In fifteenth-century Tirupati, *rahasya* means something else—a glimpse into the private sphere of erotic experience and its subjective meanings.

2. *The Padam Corpus*

Approximately thirteen thousand of Annamayya's poems were inscribed, perhaps even during his lifetime, on some 2,289 copper plates[33] that were kept in a vaultlike room in the temple, the so-called *saṅkīrtana-bhāṇḍāra.*[34] By the time of the Vijayanagara king Acyutaraya (1530), rituals were performed outside this room with the help of an endowment made for this purpose by Annamayya's eldest son, Peda Tirumalâcārya.[35] The process of inscribing thousands of poems on copper plates was definitely long

33. This, according to Gauripeddi Ramasubbasarma in his introduction to vol. 5, 52. The total number of copper plates with works by the Tāllapāka family poets is 2691 according to the official count of the Devasthanam.

34. Surviving *padams* have been published as a result of major scholarly efforts beginning in 1922. The latest complete set, reissued in 1998 from editions published over a period of some sixty years, comprises twenty-nine volumes. We have used this Devasthanam edition for our text.

35. Sadhu Subrahmanya Sastry, *Report on the Inscriptions of the Devasthanam Collections,* 285; text in V. Vijayaraghavacharya, vol. 4, *Inscriptions of Acyutāraya's Time, from 1530 A.D. to 1542 A.D.* (Madras: Tirumala Tirupati Devasthanams, 1936), no. 6 (T.T. 589), 14–19. For further mention of the *bhāṇḍāra* in inscriptions, see ibid., no. 155 (T.T. 682), 285–87; idem, vol. 5, *Inscriptions of Sadāśivarāya's Time, from 1541 A.D. to 1574 A.D.* (Madras: Tirumala Tirupati Devasthanams, 1937), no. 47 (T.T. 681), 104–11, describing the worship of the plates themselves; ibid., no. 99 (G.T. 354), 285–304.

and costly—possibly the most expensive publishing venture in the history of premodern South Asia—and reveals something of the affluence that was generated around Annamayya's name.[36]In some cases the names of the engravers[37] are recorded on the plates, and plate 5 tells us that Peda Tirumalâcārya himself sponsored the entire enterprise. An inscription repeatedly recorded in the plates tells us that Annamayya (Annamâcāryulu) began composing in the Sālivāhana year 1346 (= 1424 CE) at the age of sixteen, when the god appeared to him, and continued to compose until the twelfth day of the dark half of Phālguna in Sālivāhana 1424 (= 1503 CE)—possibly the date of his death, although the inscription does not say this explicitly.[38]

Copper plates inscribed with Tāḷḷapāka *padams* have turned up elsewhere as well—in temples at Srirangam, Ahobilam, Kadiri, Cidambaram, and Simhacalam. In addition, some *padams* that belong in this corpus have been preserved in manuscripts in the Sarasvati Mahal Library at Tanjavur, in Pudukottai, and in the Tāḷḷapāka family homes in Tirupati.[39] Arcakam Udayagiri Srinivasacaryulu, one of the finest scholars to have worked on the Tāḷḷapāka corpus, also discovered *padams* inscribed with *svara* musical notation on two rocks in the temple compound.[40] The diffusion of additional copies of *padams* on copper plates, probably beginning in the sixteenth century, attests to a process of increasing circulation, first perhaps in temples in the immediate vicinity of Tirupati and then in Vishṇu shrines throughout south India. There is clear evidence that copper plates inscribed with the songs were bound together in bunches of five, held in place by a thick ring *(kaḍiyamu)*, and carried on poles by bearers, apparently with singers following.[41] We may assume that these heavy plates achieved an iconic value as the songs spread throughout temple towns in the south. It should also be noted that Annamayya himself composed songs in praise of

36. For a discussion of the technique of engraving the plates, see Gauripeddi Ramasubbasarma's introduction to vol. 5, 56.

37. For example, Annamarāju Timmayya, at the command of Tirumalayya (see introduction to vol. 4).

38. Text of the inscription at the start of each volume. There is some ambiguity about the first date, which could perhaps be read as the date of the poet's birth.

39. See Arcakam Udayagiri Srinivasacaryulu's introduction to vol. 9, iv–v. Subbarāmadīkṣitulu's *Saṅgīta-sampradāya-pradarśini* (1901; rep., Hyderabad: Andhra Pradesh Sangita Nataka Akademy, 1974), includes two Cinnayya *padams* apparently collected from oral performance.

40. Arcakam Udayagiri Srinivasacaryulu, op. cit., iii.

41. Arcakam Udayagiri Srinivasacaryulu, introduction to vol. 10, pp. 29–30. The Ahobilam plates—35 in number, and considerably larger than the Tirupati variety—were all bound in such bunches of five.

forms of Vishṇu in various other temples, far from Tirupati—in Kadapa town, Ogunutala, Kona, and Mudiyamu in Kadapa District, Sambatturu in Kurnool District, and the Viṭṭhala shrine at Pandharpur.[42] There are also *padams* praising Govindarāja-Vishṇu, Veṅkaṭeśvara's elder brother, in Tirupati, at the foot of the hill.[43] Cina Tirumalâcārya, Peda Tirumalâcārya's son (Annamayya's grandson), has left an inscription arranging for singing of the poems in the Narasiṃhasāami temple at Mangalagiri, in Guntur District.[44] In short, we can glimpse a pattern of diffusion and institutionalization that went hand in hand with the production of the copper plates at Tirupati and that led to widespread ritual use of the songs in temples far beyond the original core area in Rayalasima.

Annamayya himself refers at least twice to the writing down of his songs: "You make me say those syllables," he tells the god, "and you make me write them down."[45] The second reference seems clearly to describe the production of the copper plates and their home inside the temple:

These are the prayers I sang at your feet,
the flowers of your fame.
Keep them with you.

Even one poem should be enough
to make you care for me.
Let the rest of them lie in your treasury.
Your name that is endless
is cheap to buy
but worth a lot.
You're my haven,
and you're there for me.
Those poems are all my wealth.

Let them lie in your treasury.[46]

42. For Kaḍapa Veṅkaṭeśvara, see SCP 308, 11:26–27, also SCP 370, 11:239–40, SCP 394, 11:323; for Kaḍpa Rāyaḍu, SCP 349, 11:167 and 168, also SCP 384, 11:287–88; for Ogunutala, SCP 365, 11:221; for Kona, SCP 371, 11:243; for Mudiyamu, SCP 324, 11:80; for Sambatturu, SCP 327, 11:93; for Pandharpur, SCP, 11:245–46.

43. SCP 396, 11:330; ACP 96, 1:320–21.

44. South Indian Inscriptions (Madras: Government Press, 1923) 4, no. 710; see Arcakam Udayagiri Srinivasacaryulu, introduction to vol. 11, 1.

45. ACP 157, 2:180.

46. ACP 169, 2:225.

"Treasury" is *bhāṇḍāramu*, probably the *saṅkīrtana-bhāṇḍāra* where the plates were stored. Does this *padam* register some mild disapproval of the process of saving the poems in this dark vault? Was it composed during the long business of inscribing and preserving what must originally have been spontaneous musical creations?

A strong modern tradition, repeated everywhere in the vast Annamayya secondary literature, states that the *padams* lying in the treasury were lost or forgotten for centuries. A person sometimes identified as the well-known scholar Veturi Prabhakara Sastri (who later did serious work on the corpus) is supposed to have found the copper plates by a dramatic accident and to have brought them back to the light of day. There is, however, no real evidence for this drama, which may simply recapitulate the common south Indian pattern relating to "sacred" texts; such texts always have to be lost and then recovered, usually only in part.[47] The story of recovery thus fits nicely into the whole pattern of ongoing hagiographic institutionalization, with its economic concomitants. Sadhu Subrahmanya Sastry, the Devasthanam epigraphist in the 1920s, tells us that he himself transported the plates "from their original place of actual concealment" to the Devasthanam office at that time.[48] They now rest in the museum run by the Devasthanam in Tirupati.

3. *The Hagiography*

Today what passes for knowledge about Annamayya comes almost entirely from a poetic biography composed by his grandson, Tāḷḷapāka Cinnanna (Cina Tiruveṅgaḷanātha), the *Annamâcārya-caritramu*. The biography belongs to a stage in which Annamayya and his poetic corpus were being

47. See discussion in D. Shulman, "Remaking a Purāṇa: The Rescue of Gajendra in Potana's Telugu *Mahābhāgavatamu*," in *Purāṇa Perennis: Reciprocity and Transformation in Hindu and Jaina Texts*, ed. W. Doniger, 122 (Albany: State University of New York Press, 1993).

In 1816 the linguist A. D. Campbell reports from Fort St. George, Madras: "Having heard that a number of poems, engraved on some thousand sheets of copper, had been preserved by the pious care of a family of Brahmins in the temple on the sacred hill at Tripetty, I deputed a native for the purpose of examining them; but, with the exception of a treatise on Grammar, of which a copy was taken, the whole collection was found to contain nothing but voluminous hymns in praise of the diety [sic]." A. D. Campbell, *A Grammar of the Teloogoo Language* (Madras: College of Fort St. George Press, 1816), xv. Thus, at the start of the nineteenth century the existence of the Tirupati copper plates was well known, and the official text of these "voluminous hymns" was easily accessible in the temple.

48. Sadhu Subrahmanya Sastry, *Tirupati Sri Venkatesvara* (Tirupati: Tirumala Tirupati Devasthanams, 1981), 242.

institutionalized at Tirupati; the poet's family and descendants, by now very wealthy as a result of Annamayya's historic function in the temple, continued to play a role in the ritual, economic, and artistic domains. We know from an inscription of 1540, for example, that Cina Tirumalâcārya, the grandson who composed the *Saṅkīrtana-lakṣaṇamu*, renovated the temple of Kalyāṇa Veṅkaṭeśvara at Śrīnivāsa-maṅgāpuram, at the foot of the mountain, and had an image of his grandfather the poet installed there, together with images of the god, the goddess Alamelumanga, and earlier south Indian Vaisnava poets and teachers.[49] The iconic series speaks eloquently of the crystallizing vision of Annamayya as an orthodox Śrīvaishṇava poet, latest and perhaps most gifted in the line going back to the Tamil Āḻvār poets and including also the great *ācārya* philosophers such as Rāmânuja. Eventually, Annamayya came to be seen as a reincarnation of Nammāḻvār, the outstanding poetic voice in the Tamil Śrīvaishṇava canon.[50] This hagiographic re-imagination or canonization of Annamayya, which does considerable violence to the unique historical context which really shaped him, has by now thoroughly established itself in Tirupati, as in South India generally. In any case, the Tāḷḷapāka family maintained their status in the temple and their investment in the Annamayya legend right up to modern times.[51]

Here, in summary, is what Cinnanna reports about his grandfather:

> Annamayya was born into a family of Nandavarīka Brahmins in Tāḷḷapāka[52] in the Pŏttapi Nāḍu, in the month of Vaiśākha, under the Viśākha star. Viṣhṇu himself told the child's father to name him Annamayya, after the Upaniṣadic verse: *annam brahmeti vyajanāt*. Already as a baby, Annamayya was focused on the god; he would cry, no matter how many lullabies were sung to him, until he heard Vishṇu's name. He sang to the god from a young age.

49. TTD series 4, no. 144: Arcakam Udayagiri Srinivasacaryulu, preface to vol. 10, 23–24.

50. See A. K. Ramanujan, *Hymns for the Drowning: Poems for Vishṇu by Nammāḻvār* (Princeton: Princeton University Press, 1981). Annamayya and Nammalvar are said to have been born under the same Visakha asterism.

51. George Stratton, British collector at Chittor in 1803, noted that the Tāḷḷapāka family were still singing in the temple. See Sanjay Subrahmanyam, *Penumbral Visions: Making Polities in Early Modern South* India (Delhi: Oxford University Press, 2001), 24, and sources cited there.

52. In Kadapa District, Rajampeta Taluk. Cinnanna tells us that the Nine Nāth Siddhas (*nava-nātha-siddhulu*) achieved the ability to make base metal into gold (*rasa-siddhi*) there; *Srītāllapaka annamâcāryula jīvita-caritramu*, edited with introduction by Veturi Prabhakara Sastri; reedited by Gauripeddi Ramasubbasarma (Tirupati: Devasthanam, 1978), 4.

One day his sister-in-law sent the young idle boy to bring grass for the cows. Taking a handful of grass in his hand, he cut it with a sickle—and at the same time cut his little finger. He cried out, "Hari Hari!" This was the moment of transformation. Throwing away the sickle, and cutting his bonds to his family and teacher—for god himself was both teacher and family to him—Annamayya joined a band of pilgrims headed for Veṅkaṭam hill.

With them, he walked to Tirupati and began to climb the hill. On the way up he stopped to worship at a village goddess shrine (*śakti-guḍi*) of the shepherds.[53] From there he visited the Talayeru rock. It was late morning, and he was hungry, actually blinded by hunger; he had never left his mother before. He lay down, wearing his sandals, under a bamboo bush, on a flat slab of rock. The goddess of Tirupati, Alamelumanga came to him, for she knew he was hungry; milk oozed from her breasts, and she offered him a stream of delicious compassion (*kṛpâmṛta-dhāra*). She told him to remove his sandals, since the mountain was covered with holy *sālagrāma* stones. As he did so, he saw the mountain fully, in its deep golden hue. She fed him from the *prasāda* that she and Vishṇu ate together in the temple.

At once, poetry came to the boy, and he composed a *śataka* (one hundred verses) for Alamelumanga. He bathed in the Koneru tank, bowed to the god in his shrine, and offered him a coin (a *kāsu* tied to his *dhoti*). The next day he sang another *śataka*, this time to Veṅkaṭeśvara himself, whose marks the boy inscribed on his body. When Annamayya recited his long poem before the locked doors of the temple, they opened to admit him. Inside, he recited the *śataka* again in the presence of the Nambi priest; a pearl necklace fell from above, a gift of the god.

In the temple Annamayya was initiated by a Vaishṇava renouncer, to whom the god had appeared in a dream, announcing the arrival of this dark young boy to receive the Vaishṇava signs (the conch and discus). The sage then sent Annamayya back home, where soon he was married to two young girls, Tirumalamma (= Timmakka) and Akkalamma. The girls' relatives at first objected to this match: "How can one marry a daughter to someone

53. According to Veturi Prabhakari Sastri in the introduction to Cinnanna's text, 7, this *śakti* is Tāḷḷapāka Gaṅgamma, the Tirupati goddess. See below, section 4. Prabhakara Sastri says that this Tāḷḷapāka Gaṅgamma is the Tirupati *kṣetra-devatā* and is worshiped by pilgrims before they climb the mountain to see Veṅkaṭeśvara—just as Annamayya is said to have done.

so unworldly?" But the god came in a dream to the girls' parents and arranged the match.

After the wedding, the god of Ahobilam—Vishṇu as Narasiṃha—arrived in the form of a guru and gave the bridegroom the discus and a *mantra*. The god Hayagrīva also appeared before him. From another teacher, Śaṭhakopa-muni, who followed the tradition of Vedântadeśika,[54] Annamayya learned Vedānta. He studied the *Vālmīki-rāmāyaṇa* with deep feeling. Gradually he became known beyond his home as a composer of songs.

The king, Sāḷuva Narasiṃha, ruler of Tanguturu (before he assumed high position in Vijayanagara), sought out the young man and asked him to join him and support him—as Kṛṣṇa supported Arjuna. Annamayya followed this king, first to Tanguturu, with its Keśava temple, then to Penugonda. The king showered gifts upon him—a headdress, bracelets, two parasols, a pair of whisks, a spittoon, and a house next to the king's. One day, in the royal court, the king invited Annamayya to sing, and the poet sang the famous *padam "emŏkŏ ciguruṭadharamuna"*:

These marks of black musk
on her lips, red as buds,
what are they but letters of love
sent by our friend to her lover?

Her eyes the eyes of a *cakora* bird,
why are they red in the corners?

Think it over, my friends:
what is it but the blood
still staining the long glances
that pierced her beloved
after she drew them from his body
back to her eyes?

What are they but letters of love?

How is it that this woman's breasts
show so bright through her sari?

54. *Sarva-tantra-svatantra-sampradāya.*

Can't you guess, my friends?
It's the rays from the crescents
left by the nails of her lover
rays luminous as moonlight on a summer night?

What are they but letters of love?

What are these graces,
these pearls,
raining down her cheeks?

Can't you imagine, friends?
What could they be but beads of sweat
left on her gentle face
by the god on the hill
when he pressed hard,
frantic in love?

What are they but letters of love?[55]

The king asked him to sing the *padam* again and again, saying, "This is true poetry." But in his blindness and pride, he then demanded that the poet compose a *padam* like this one—about him. Annamayya, horrified, covered his ears; in the mode of total faithfulness that is exemplified by a good wife, he said to the king, "The tongue that sings to god will not praise you. Singing to anyone other than Vishṇu would be as terrible as sleeping with a sister. I can't accept you, and I don't want your friendship. I'll go back to my god." So the king had his soldiers arrest Annamayya. "I brought you here and gave you riches, because you are my childhood friend. Now I asked for one word, and you're upset." Annamayya was sent to jail, bound by three strong chains.

The poet sang to the god:

When they put you in chains,
or order you killed,
when your creditors squeeze you,

55. SCP 14, 5:57. See V. Narayana Rao, A. K. Ramanujan, and D. Shulman, *When God Is a Customer: Telugu Courtesan Songs by Kṣetrayya and Others* (Berkeley and Los Angeles: University of California Press, 1993), 49–50.

only *his* name will get you out.
Stubborn as you are,
there is no other way.[56]

The chains fell away. The guards hastened to inform the king, who came to the jail and ordered Annamayya chained again, in iron so heavy that two guards had to carry it. Again the poet sang his poem, and the chain broke in pieces around his toe. The king wept, bowed at his feet, and sought forgiveness; he gave gifts to Annamayya and carried him himself in his palankeen.

Annamayya left Penugonda and returned to Venkatam, where he sang, over the years, thirty-two thousand *saṅkīrtanalu* to the god—some in Yoga, some in the erotic *śṛṅgāra* mode, some in the *vairāgya* mode of renunciation. He also composed a *Rāmāyaṇa*, in *dvipada;* a *Veṅkaṭâdri-māhātmya*, in Sanskrit; and twenty-three *śatakas* and many *prabandhas* in various languages. He raised his own family to be poets. He had the gift of blessing or cursing, for he had acquired purity of the tongue; people put his sandals on their heads to win relief from distress. The god himself appeared to him and said, "When Krishnamâcārya [the author of the *Siṃhagiri-vacanamulu*] sang to me in the metaphysical genre *(adhyātma)*, I became detached *(virakta);* but when you sang the love-songs of *śṛṅgāra*, I became a young man *(mañci-prāyambuvāḍu)*."[57]

Such is the story which, as a whole, aligns Annamayya with the classical south Indian Śrīvaishṇava image of a pious saint. Like his predecessor Nammāḻvār, the child is born with love for Vishṇu in his heart. As a young boy he actualizes this devotion—after being thrown out of the house as a useless idler by his sister-in-law—by a spontaneous pilgrimage to Tirupati where, nursed by the goddess herself, he begins his literary career. Divine qualities animate him from the beginning, and his poems are inspired by—actually they are another form of—the breastmilk that the goddess feeds him. He does, however, marry (two wives) and assume a householder's role, still singing for the god. He is not a "renouncer"—although, as we shall see, his so-called *adhyātma* poems often express great hostility to life in the

56. *Ākaṭi-velalan…saṅkĕlal' iduvela:* ACP 26, 1:107.

57. *Śrītāḷḷapāka annamâcāryula jīvita-caritramu*, edited with introduction by Veturi Prabhakara Sastri, reedited by Gauripeddi Ramasubbasarma (Tirupati: Devasthanam, 1978). The text concludes with various miraculous achievements of the poet and also mentions that he treated the Kannada poet Purandara-dāsa as an incarnation of Viṭṭhala/Vishṇu (at Pandharpur). Purandara-dāsa sang of Annamayya, though it is not clear if they are thought to have met.

world and, especially, to women. These latter poems are no doubt what Cinnanna means by the "*vairāgya* mode of renunciation."

A moment of overt conflict arises when the king, Sāḷuva Narasimha, before his elevation to the Vijayanagara throne, attempts to co-opt the poet into the classic courtly role of singing to the god-king. This fusion of royal and divine aspects is a standard feature of Nāyaka-period states, as we have shown at length elsewhere.[58] Its appearance in Cinnanna's text, from the mid-sixteenth century, anticipates this development and also dates the retrospective biography. As the prototypical Vaiṣṇava devotee, Annamayya must, of course, refuse to cooperate with the king. One of the *padams*, probably a general description of human distress, is conscripted to tell a story of release from iron chains.

Nevertheless, despite the severe patterning evident in this biography, the grandson has chosen a particularly beautiful *padam* of the erotic type to make his point about the nature of Annamayya's vision. The goddess is emerging from her bedroom as her girlfriends tease her about the telltale signs on her body. Each of the images is complex. Her red eyes are stained with the blood drawn from her lover's body by her penetrating glances. The moon-shaped marks *(nakha-rekha)* left by his nails on her breasts radiate like moonlight itself *(śaśi-rekha)*; thus, the simile becomes literally real. This movement toward the concrete dominates the whole poem. In the end, we have the pearl-like beads of sweat—left by the god on the woman's face when he made love. But along with this extreme concretization, a certain distancing comes into effect with the realization that the woman is not just any woman. She is god's wife, as the climax of the poem tells us explicitly. Hence the listener cannot simply relate to her as to the *nāyikā*-heroine of a classical, *rasa*-style erotic poem. He/she comes to know her as a goddess and, from this vantage point, participates in her experience. This mode allows him to approach the god intimately and passionately. Here is Sāḷ uva Narasimha's "mistake": he chooses *to be god* in this context and thinks of the woman as potentially his consort. Thus, Cinnanna's choice of this *padam* points both to a real historical conflict and to an evolution in mode: it enables a critical distinction between this poet's devotional love-poetry and the classical legacy of courtlystyle *śṛṅgāra* poems.

But we should not stop here. Neither of the two types just mentioned—*bhakti* erotics or courtly *śṛṅgāra*—really captures the uniqueness of Annamayya's achievement. There is a third option for reading, probably even more real in Annamayya's own time than it was for his successors. These

58. V. Narayana Rao, David Shulman, and Sanjay Subrahmanyam, *Symbols of Substance: Court and State in Nāyaka Period Tamil Nadu* (Delhi: Oxford University Press, 1992).

padams are love-poems of a new type—entirely human, individualized, unrestrained. Listening to such a poem, the reader, like the poet himself, may become aware that the woman in question is the goddess, and that her lover is Lord Veṅkaṭeśvara. He or she may also even bring to bear, for a moment, associations evoked by the classical *nāyaka* and *nāyikā* of the courts. None of this disturbs the fact that what the reader is taking in, as the *padam* unfolds and repeats, is a highly subjective love-poem largely resistant to classification in the familiar categories. The erotic expressivity of such a poem need not be constrained or limited to what we like to call "devotion," on the one hand, or classical *śṛṅgāra*, on the other. The real challenge to the reader lies precisely in this rather new and unexpected openness. In this respect, a vast gap divides Annamayya from a devotional classic such as Jayadeva's *Gīta-govinda;* at the same time, Annamayya's love-poems easily extend into the bold idiom of Kṣetrayya in the seventeenth-century and later *padam* authors in both Telugu and Tamil.[59]

4. *Tāḷḷapāka Origins*

Cinnanna's "biography" belongs, as we have said, to the stage in which Annamayya himself, together with his family, was being canonized at the very temple that the Tāḷḷapāka poets had helped to refashion in the form we know it today. Annamayya, that is, like the god Veṅkaṭeśvara himself, has been "Veṅkaṭeśvarized," his image rendered normative, beneficent, and supremely pacific in line with the pious, elevated *(sāttivka)* values of medieval Tamil Śrīvaishṇavism. There is, however, a strong surviving tradition, widely attested in Tirupati and studied by scholars such as Gopalakrsna Abburi and Allamaraju Viyayendranatha Ravu, which places the origins of Annamayya's Tāḷḷapāka family in an altogether different milieu. These Nandavarīka Brahmins are said to have come from Nandavaram, between Banaganipalle and Panyam in today's Kurnool District of Rayalasima to the north and west of Tirupati. Nanda, the king of this town, wanted to go to Benares, far away to the north, to bathe in the Ganges each day. The Siddha Dattātreya gave him sandals that allowed him to go through an

59. See *When God Is a Customer*, 9–20. For the opposition of temple poets to court poets, see V. Narayana Rao and D. Shulman, *Classical Telugu Poetry: An Anthology* (Berkeley and Los Angeles: University of California Press, 2002), 43–47; V. Narayana Rao, "Multiple Literary Cultures in Telugu: Court, Temple, and Public," in *Literary Cultures in History: Reconstructions from South Asia*, ed. Sheldon Pollock (Berkeley and Los Angeles: University of California Press, 2003), 383–436.

underground tunnel to the holy city, so each morning he would traverse the tunnel, bathe, and return. But one day his wife discovered that he was missing in the morning and, when she later forced him to explain, demanded to be allowed to join him the next day. So the couple went to Benares together and took their bath. But on the way back, the queen's *mantras* failed (some say, because she was menstruating), and she was stuck. The king stayed with her out of loyalty. He begged the Brahmins of Benares to help him, and they agreed on condition that he would protect them at some later date, when need arose. He promised this in the presence of the goddess Cāmuṇḍeśvari, at the Cāmuṇḍeśvari Ghat. With the Brahmins' help, he and his queen then returned home.

Years later, famine struck and the Brahmins came to Nandavaram to ask the king to make good on his promise. He denied everything and asked which god could bear witness to the Brahmins' claim. They returned to Benares and asked the goddess to bear witness. She agreed to follow them to Nandavaram on condition that they not look back to see if she was with them. They successfully fulfilled this condition, and Cāmuṇḍeśvari then faced the king and demanded that he fulfill his promise. At the Brahmins' request, the goddess stayed with them in Nandavaram—and that is why the Cāmuṇḍeśvari temple in Benares no longer has an image in the sanctum.

A certain Niyogi Brahmin, one Duggana Appayya, followed this group of Brahmins from Benares, but they, being Vaidikis, refused to accept his daughter as a bride for any of their sons. In despair, the Niyogi killed himself and his whole family and became a Brahmin demon. (Another version of the story says that he cursed the Nandavarīka Brahmins to suffer permanent amnesia, which is why they no longer remember their origins.)[60] At this point the goddess—now called Cauḍeśvari—also cursed the Brahmins, who had caused the death of another Brahmin, to live by worldly jobs and to serve as priests for the meat-eating Tŏgaṭa weavers. These Brahmins are the Nandavarīkas, from whom the Tāḷḷapāka people came.[61]

60. Allamaraju Viyajendranatha Ravu, *Tĕlugu sāhityamlo cauḍeśvarī-devi caritra* (Kurnool: privately printed, 1999), 161. The Nandavarīka Brahmins still blame the goddess and her curse when they happen to forget something.

61. See Gauripeddi Ramasubbasarma, introduction to vol. 5, 3–6, citing the *Cauḍeśvari-māhātmyamu* of Gaunipallĕ Rāmappakavi (unfortunately unavailable to us). For a richly detailed study of these materials, see Viyajendranatha Ravu, *Tĕlugu sāhityamlo cauḍeśvarī-devi caritra*. See also E. Thurston, *Castes and Tribes of Southern India* (Madras: 1909) 8:170–71, s.v. Tŏgaṭa. Gopalakrsna Abburi has also studied the Nandavarīka origin myth in its relation to the weaver communities. See *Śrī Annamâcāryulu, yakṣagāna sampradāyam* (Hyderabad: Abburi Trust, 2002), 19–62.

Cauḍeśvari is still a living presence in Tirupati and the surrounding areas. A corpus of popular *Cauḍamma padālu* narrates her story, including this legend.[62] It has a complexity worthy of the Tāḷḷapāka materials and may help us understand some of the more unusual aspects of Annamayya's poetry. Note the empty shrine in Benares and the Eurydice-like goddess who follows faithfully if you don't look back; also the profoundly ambiguous status of the amnesiac Nandavarīka Brahmins and their close relations with the weaver community. If we take the story as seriously as it deserves, we discover that this family was originally linked to the cult of a local goddess, probably in Tallapaka. In fact, Annamayya's grandson, Cina Tirumalâcārya, suggests precisely some such "dark" origin for the family:

paccitāmasula mammu parama-sātvikulagā
yiccaṭane sesināḍu yĕnta citramu
yiccagiñci mākulānan ennaḍu leni vaiṣṇavam'
accamuga gṛpa sesĕn annamâcāryuḍu

We were engaged in totally dark rituals
and Annamacarya made us bright.
What an amazing feat!
There was no Vaishṇava worship in our family
before he gave it to us in his kindness.[63]

These "totally dark rituals" are almost certainly connected to the worship of a goddess like the meat-eating Cauḍeśvari. Such rituals tend to be passionate, palpably physical, intensely colorful and dramatic, and often include experiences of possession by the goddess. In such extreme states, the subject speaks in altered voices and seemingly alien personae—the voice of the goddess herself, perhaps resonating with elements in the personality and biography of the possessed.

More evidence of a link between the Tāḷḷapāka family and a village goddess (this time in Tāḷḷapāka village) is preserved in the opening section of Cinnanna's hagiography, cited above. Annamayya's grandfather, Nārāyaṇa, was a poor student, constantly punished severely by his teacher—beaten,

62. Gurram Sarvayya, *Cauḍamma Padālu*, ed. Pappuru Cinna Cauḍappa (Simhadripuram, Kadapa District: Pappuru Pedda Cauḍappa and Pappuru Kadirappa, 1976). According to the *Cāmuṇḍikā-vilāsamu* of Raṅgayâmātyuni Rāmakṛṣṇa-kavi, an eighteenth-century Nandavarīka poet, the goddess informed the Nandavarīkas that since she wanted to eat meat in the Kali-yuga, her worship should be transferred to the hands of the Tŏgaṭa weavers; details in Vijayendranātha Ravu, *Tĕlugu sāhityamlo cauḍeśvarī-devi caritra*, 191–92.

63. ACP 9 of Cina Tirumalâcārya, 10:29–30.

made to hang from a rope tied to the ceiling with a mass of thorns below him, and so on. In despair, he ran to the goddess Cintālamma's temple, since he had heard that in the anthill behind the shrine there was a deadly snake. The unhappy boy thrust his hand into the anthill in the hope of being bitten. At that moment the goddess, who knows past, present, and future, appeared to him in her own form and asked him why he wanted to die. "I'm tired of being beaten by my teacher," said the boy. The goddess advised, "Bow to Lord Vishṇu in the village, and he will bestow learning on you. Moreover, in the third generation from now, a great devotee of Vishṇu will be born."[64] In this small episode that has survived inside the canonical life-story of our poet, the very continuity of the Tāḷḷapāka line depends entirely on intervention by a village goddess. The original connection between this family and the goddess was too strong to be obliterated from collective memory.

According to Annamayya's grandson, the Tāḷḷapāka family made the transition to a *sāttvika* Vaishṇava mode of worship within a single generation, in the lifetime of Annamayya himself.[65] But even today the Tirupati religious complex as a whole is a configuration of these two intertwined and complementary religious systems—one related to Veṅkaṭeśvara, on the hill, and his brother Govindarāja, down below, the other deeply connected to local goddesses such as Cauḍeśvari, Gaṅgamma, and the more *sāttvika* Padmāvati/Alamelumaṅga in her Mangapuram temple. These two systems appear to be very distinct, but, in fact, each has influenced the other profoundly. There is a stubborn local tradition that Veṅkaṭeśvara himself was originally a goddess, converted simultaneously to Śrīvaishṇavism and to maleness by the philosopher Rāmânuja; the particularly graceful left hand of the Veṅkaṭeśvara stone image is said to be a remnant of this primordial feminine identity.[66] In this case, maleness would be little more than an external guise imposed from without (by an authoritative, Brahmin man) on the god; his persistent problem, one might say, would be to find a way for the inner reality, which was and remains female, somehow to come through. Lest this notion seem entirely exotic, we refer to the cult of Gaṅgamma at Tirupati. Here, every year, the goddess goes through a series of guises, *veṣālu*, including one as a prince *(dora)* and his minister, only to peel off

64. Cinnanna, *Śrītāḷḷapāka annamâcāryula jīvita-caritramu*, 6–7.

65. Allamaraju Vijayendranatha Ravu places the ritual shift from Nandavarīkas to Tŏgaṭas as goddess priests in the early fifteenth century. See *Tĕlugu sāhityamlo cauḍeśvarī-devi caritra*, 193.

66. Cf. N. Ramesan, *The Tirumala Temple* (Tirupati: Tirumala Tirupati Devasthanams, 1981), 116–17.

maleness as a superfluous obstruction that hides the more alive, more real female innerness.[67] Male participants in the Gangamma cult go through a similar process, often assuming complete female dress in the course of the annual *jātra*.

Such conceptions are deep-seated, pervasive, and well integrated into the Tirupati cultic world seen as a complex, interlocking whole. They may have constituted the natural conceptual matrix out of which the Tāḷḷapāka phenomenon emerged. Certainly, something of this fascination with feminine identity, in specific senses—especially the notion of a deeper or hidden femininity—comes through in the *"śṛṅgāra" padams*. We will return to this theme.

5. *The God Who Pays Interest*

We know from an inscription that a *Tiruveṅkaṭa-māhātmya*, containing the mythic biography of Veṅkaṭeśvara, was composed or publicly performed in 1491.[68] Although we cannot identify this text with any of the surviving, rich *purāṇic* materials from Tirupati,[69] much evidence points to a period of intense creativity in this domain in the fifteenth and sixteenth centuries, that is, roughly the high period of Tāḷḷapāka literary and intellectual activity. By this point the Pāñcarātra-based, goddess-oriented ritual system had been assimilated to the temple's annual cycle, which must have crystallized more or less as we know it today. No less important, a new story about Veṅkaṭeśvara made its appearance and came eventually to subsume much earlier mythic materials.[70] This story reflects an important shift in the social composition and economic profile of the Tirupati area in the fifteenth century. At its heart lies the rise of so-called "left-hand" castes, not directly tied to the land—artisans, merchant-traders, herders—and a gradual monetariza-

67. See Don Handelman, "The Guises of the Goddess and the Transformation of the Male: Gangamma's Visit to Tirupati and the Continuum of Gender," in *Syllables of Sky: Studies in South Indian Civilization in honour of Velcheru Narayana Rao*, ed. D. Shulman (Delhi: Oxford University Press, 1995), 293–37. Joyce B. Flueckiger is preparing a monograph on Gaṅgamma in Tirupati.

68. Sadhu Subrahmanya Sastry and V. Vijayaraghavacharya, eds., *Inscriptions of Sāḷuva Narasimha's Time, from 1445 A.D. to 1504 A.D.* (Madras: Tirumala Tirupati Devasthanams, 1984), no. 95 (T.T. 253), 193–98. The author of this text was apparently one Pasindi Veṅkaṭatturṟaaivar.

69. Compiled most usefully in the *Śrīveṅkaṭâcala-māhātmya*, a collection of various unrelated Sanskrit *māhātmya* texts on the temple, published by the Devasthanam in 1847.

70. We can only hint here at the results of a more detailed analysis of the *purāṇic* sources from Tirupati, still in progress.

tion and development of a cash economy. Within this new configuration of social and economic space, with related developments in the political and institutional sphere,[71] the temple came to assume a prominent role as magnet and manager of resources, both symbolic and concrete, while the god in its innermost chamber became something between an emperor and a large-scale (but also rather needy) banker.

We have called this process at Tirupati "Veṅkaṭeśvarization"—the re-imagining of the deity in his full-fledged Veṅkaṭeśvara persona as the "god on the hill" or the "lord of the seven hills." As such, this god has certain relatively recent attributes: he is *Vaḍḍikāsulavāḍu* or *Vaṭṭi paṇam pĕrumāḷ*, "the god who pays interest on a loan." The local Sanskrit *purāṇas* explain this title by the following story. Vishṇu came to Tirupati in a state of shocking loneliness; Lakshmī, his feminine part, insulted by his response to a certain incident, had left him and hidden herself on earth (at Kolhapur in Maharastra). The god was searching for her, wandering through the world until he happened upon Venkatam Hill at Tirupati. Here he felt a certain relief. He rented a room on the mountain from Varāha, the Boar—that is, from himself, Vishṇu, in an earlier form. The written agreement between these two deities is still preserved in the Varāha-svāmi temple on top of the hill, which pilgrims are supposed to visit before entering Veṅkaṭeśvara's shrine. Eventually Veṅkaṭeśvara fell in love with a local girl, Padmāvati, the daughter of the king, Ākāśa-rāja ("King of All Space"). After protracted negotiations, including a tantalizing exchange of letters between the prospective bridegroom and the girl's father, Veṅkaṭeśvara married Padmāvati. However, as is well known, weddings cost quite a lot of money, and the god could hardly ask his first (and absent) wife, Lakshmī, to cover the expenses, so he was reduced to taking a loan from Kubera, the banker of the goddess. (Oral tradition at Tirupati insists that the loan came from Govindarāja, Veṅkaṭeśvara's elder brother, who lies resting in his temple in the town.) The loan came at very high interest; as a result, pilgrims who climb the hill at Tirupati encounter a huge collection box *(huṇḍi)* on their way into the temple, where they can help the god with his interest payments. As to the principal of the loan, its repayment will come only in some future age.[72]

71. In particular, inscriptions reveal the growth in power of the mutts and of a series of prominent mediators between the kings and the temple apparatus. See A. Appadurai, *Worship and Conflict under Colonial Rule: A South Indian Case* (Cambridge: Cambridge University Press, 1981), 85–101.

72. This compressed version of the story of Veṅkaṭeśvara's wedding follows chapters 5–11 of the text that refers to itself as *Śrīveṅkaṭâcala-māhātmya* from *Bhaviṣyottara-purāṇa*, in the collection mentioned in n. 69 above. Parts of the story run parallel to *Veṅkaṭâcala-māhātmya* in vol. 2 of the printed *Skanda-purāṇa* (Bombay: Venkatesvara Steam Press).

The story clearly conveys the new ethos of written contracts, loans, investments, and entrepreneurship—an ethos that came to dominate much of the life of this great temple. Veṅkaṭeśvara himself is driven, first, by the hopeless attempt to reconstitute his shattered wholeness, to reclaim the goddess who has abandoned him. Then this effort is channeled in the direction of Padmāvati in the new, local sphere, whose king accepts him in due course as a son-in-law and prospective heir. To this end, the god assumes the crushing burden of the loan that we, his pilgrims, share with him to this day. Notice the asymmetrical dependence of god on human beings, a theme that comes up frequently in the *padams* as well. Veṅkaṭeśvara can make his interest payments only with *our* help. Several *padams* also confirm the somewhat mercenary ethos we are describing; for example, the following love-poem, spoken (somewhat unusually) by the male lover:

What profit will you get
out of hiding from me?
I'm right here, and I want you.

Those fantastic eyes—do you want to lock them in a bank?
You don't even raise your head to look at me.
Do you think you can invest that amazing smile at a good rate?
I can't get you to smile at me.

What profit will you get?

Those towering breasts—are you going to put them in a vault?
You're hiding them under your sari.
Are you planning to hoard underground
the full bloom of your youth?
You keep so still under your veil.

What profit will you get?

You want to stash away words instead of spending them in love?
You don't even move your lips.
You belong to me now, and I—
I'm God.
At last we can do business.

What profit will you get?[73]

73. SCP 471, 12:207.

One further element needs to be noted here—the prominence of the weaver communities (Tŏgaṭa, Kaikāla, Devāṅga) in ritual contexts at Tirupati. The Tŏgaṭas appear in relation to Cauḍamma and the Nandavarīkas, whose ritual roles they are said to have inherited, as we have seen. Annamayya himself portrays Veṅkaṭeśvara as a weaver *(neta-behāri)* in one of his *padams*.[74] Kaikālas provide the main ritual node for the Gaṅgamma cult and hold the keys to the Govindarāja temple in Tirupati. There is also a specific link between the weavers and the Tāḷḷapāka family: Tirupati weavers are said to have chosen Cinnanna, Annamayya's grandson, as their *guru* and to have requested that this role remain in the hands of Cinnanna's descendents for generations.[75] The roles of the weavers are clearly congruent with the larger picture of a "left-hand" organization of the Tirupati cult system and with the values and ethos this system embodies, including the image of the indebted god weaving together the various strands of the local sociopolitical (and metaphysical) order.

To sum up the rather schematic historical argument we are suggesting:[76] We have a temple that has gone through several transformations—first brought into line with Āgamic Vaishṇavism and then "Veṅkaṭeśvarized." In the course of the first millennium CE, an orthodox Vaikhāṇasa ritual regime was established around the original local deity, perhaps a form of the boar, probably intimately linked to the goddess.[77] Royal patronage from the major political systems in this area was slowly drawn to the temple, becoming substantial in the Choḻa period (early tenth century). By the twelfth century, the goddess had successfully asserted or reasserted her rights, as we see in the incorporation of Pāñcarātra elements by the mature ritual complex and the construction of the Padmāvati/Alamelumaṅga shrine in Tiruccanur at the base of the mountain. When Tāḷḷapāka Annamayya arrived in Tirupati in the early fifteenth century, he found the temple moving toward an economic "boom," supported by various left-hand castes and their associated political and institutional structures. In the course of that century, strong ties were forged with the rising political center of Vijayanagara, at first through local rulers who took their interest in the Tirupati temple with them when they moved to the royal capital. The new profile

74. ACP 45, 1:184. See Pillalamarri Ramulu, *Telugulo bhaktikavitvam: sāmājika viśleṣaṇa* (Hyderabad: privately printed, 1999), 74.

75. Salva Krishnamurthy, ed., *The Tunes of Divinity*, xlviii. The weavers paid Cinnanna ten thousand *varāhas* at the time this relationship was formalized. See also the discussion by Gopalakrishna Abburi, in *Srī Annamâcāryulu, yakṣagāna sampradāyam*, 42–46, and sources cited there.

76. We hope to set it out fully in a separate monograph on Tirupati.

77. This linkage comes through explicitly in the Sanskrit *purāṇic* sources.

the temple assumed at this time, with the ethos of a thriving cash culture built into the very myth of Veṅkaṭeśvara, was partly achieved through the work of Annamayya himself. Annamayya modeled the highly personal relationship of the devotee to the god and gave voice to the immense range of imaginative modes through which this connection could be realized. To a large extent, his vision was shaped by the original Tāḷḷapāka milieu, with its intense relation to the local goddess and its esoteric Nāth tradition; the particular configuration of this rich Rayalasima cultic universe was successfully transplanted to Tirupati and its male god by the Tāḷḷapāka poets. By the time the Annamayya *padams* were inscribed on copper plates and diffused throughout southern Andhra and Tamil Nadu in the sixteenth century, both Annamayya himself and the god he worshiped had been radically transfigured. In a very real sense, Annamayya's poems created Veṅkaṭeśvara, the god on the hill, as we know him today. Annamayya was Veṅkaṭeśvara's court poet, and the god rewarded him and his family lavishly in the royal manner.

6. Listening to the Padams (1): Introspective Poems

A central problem for anyone reading through the Annamayya corpus is the meaning of the inherited categorical division into "metaphysical"—as noted earlier, we prefer the term "introspective"—and "love" poems, *adhyātma* and *śṛṅgāra*. As we have seen, this division is already present in the copper plates themselves. And while the placement of some *padams* in one or the other division sometimes seems a little arbitrary, the fact that the poet did work in two quite distinct modes is very clear. In fact, so distinctive are the two voices that one might at times even wonder how they can coexist in the same consciousness, although both parts of the corpus share the *padam* form and a certain characteristic quality of language.

The introspective voice tends to be tormented, conflicted, sometimes desperate, sometimes guilty and misogynist, sometimes merely wistful and sad, usually highly lyrical:

kaḍal uḍipi nīrāḍaga talacuvāralaku
kaḍaleni manasunaku gaḍama yĕkkaḍidi

dāham' aṇagina vĕnaka tatvam' ĕrigĕdan' anna
dāham' el' aṇagu tā tattvam' em' ĕrugu
dehambugala yanni dinamulaku padârtha-
moham' el' uḍugu dā mudam' ela kalugu

mundar' ĕrigina vĕnaka mŏdalu maracĕdan' anna
mundar' em' ĕrugu dā mŏdal' ela maracu
andamuga tiruveṅkaṭâdrīśu mannanala
kanduv' ĕrigina melu kalanaina ledu

You say you want to bathe
when the waves subside.
Is there an end
to the endless mind?

You say, "Let me quench my thirst,
and then I'll find the truth."
Why should thirst be quenched?
How can you know truth?

Is there an end?

All the days you have a body,
why should longing cease?
How can you find joy?

Is there an end?

You say, "After I know what lies ahead,
I'll forget what was before."
Can you know what lies ahead?
How can you forget what was before?

Is there an end?

That goodness that comes of knowing
how to reach god—
you won't find it
in your wildest dreams.

Is there an end?[78]

Like so many of the *adhyātma* poems, this one has a meditative quality, strangely familiar to us. We overhear the speaker's persistent questions; his mind is negotiating with itself, interrogating itself, carrying on an internal

78. ACP 36, 1:150–51.

discussion between two voices. The first is the voice of standard mental operation, heavy with insecurity, setting down conditions and making bargains with the world: "If you promise that what comes next will be better, I'll give up what I have now." The second voice ridicules these conditions. Reality is resistant to such bargains. The speaker who contains this dialogue knows this quite well, but still his mind cannot let go. As a result, his hopes of reaching the goodness, *melu*, "that comes of knowing how to reach god" remain unattainable. That goodness is beyond his grasp, beyond his wildest dreams, so long as his human conditioning continues to operate.

It is a gentle poem for all that, rich in soft consonants (liquids, nasals, and alveolars), built around simple questions and rhetorical answers—like the kind of dialogue that goes on all the time in anyone's mind, on the edge of awareness. Underlying the dialogue is the opening, ironic image: the ocean, like the mind, never really subsides. There *is* no end. We can imagine the dialogue continuing forever in the spiraling cycles that are built into the Telugu syntax. What this implies is that the problem is inherent in being human, if being human means having an embodied mind.

Sometimes Annamayya tells us this very directly:

> I was better off then.
> Better off in my past lives
> than in this misery.
>
> When I was born as a worm,
> at home in the mud,
> I never had these worries.
> It's much worse to be human.
> I was better off then.
>
> Born as a lowly beast,
> subject to so much pain,
> I didn't know poverty from riches.
> Now I know.
> I was better off then.
>
> Committing so many wrongs,
> I've fallen into hell.
> You were there for me.
> I was better off then.[79]

79. ACP 1, 1:3.

In many of the poems, a potential resolution of this endemic human difficulty is offered in the form of surrender, and the classical Vaishṇava term for such a move—*śaraṇâgati,* "seeking refuge"—surfaces in Annamayya's speech. But let us see what is meant by this usage here. There is an implication that this act involves a deeper, more real self:

> I don't have to get rid of it.
> I don't have to hold on to it.
> All I have to do is to be me.
> All knots will be untied.
>
> If you have god in your thoughts every day,
> you'll forget what worries you.
> Like a lemon you're clutching
> when you fall asleep,
> karma will fall away.
> You'll be free.[80]

Unfortunately, it is not so simple "to be me." The promise of resolution tends to be stated very laconically: it is there, but there may be no way to reach it. What we hear in the *adhyātma* poems is the immensity of the problems, imaginatively described in great detail. It is like reading entries in a diary, full of conflict and self-doubt and recorded in a long series of varying moods. The god is present in this continuous self-analysis—but at some distance.

Nonetheless, many of the poems are addressed directly to the god, whom the poet cajoles, taunts, ridicules, and toys with, all in the context of the intimate relationship that exists between them. The poet knows god in all his incarnations, his mythic biographies, his theological attributes (some of which he seems to mock). In such moods, the poet allows himself a tone of defiant audacity:

> Just for fun, you drown living beings
> in the ocean of life, and then you dredge them up.
> For this flaw, they make you sleep
> on the ocean, even if
> you're God.[81]

80. ACP 370, 4:278.
81. ACP 32, 1:133.

He makes the most of the god's dependence upon him, the speaker:

> Imagine that I wasn't here. What would you do with your kindness?
> You get a good name because of me.
> Think it over. By saving someone so low,
> you win praise all over the world.
> You get merit from me, and I get life
> out of you. We're right for each other,
> god on the hill.
>
> *Imagine that I wasn't here.*[82]

The verbal attack may be pointed and sarcastic:

> Are you the same crazy kid
> who stole the butter?
> You can't be seen or heard.
>
> You hold in your belly
> all those people who don't accept you.
> When the dying man said *nāra,*
> asking for coconut fibers,
> you heard it as your name, Nārāyaṇa,
> and saved him, like a hero.
>
> *Are you crazy?*[83]

The god's mostly compassionate actions appear incongruous with his dignity and power—hence the suggestion that he is crazy. This god makes himself ridiculous by rushing out to save his rather unworthy devotees, such as the speaker. On the other hand, poems like this one always have an undertone that cancels the surface meaning and conveys the true depth of intimacy and acceptance. This tone of playful connection stands in marked contrast to the diary-like confessions, so interwoven with doubt and self-reproach.

So we have the questioning voice, scanning a conflictual and unstable mental landscape, aware of the images the mind is throwing, like shadow puppets, onto the screen;[84] aware, too, of the contradictions that seem to

82. ACP 208, 3:33.
83. ACP 106, 2:22.
84. ACP 220, 3:75.

arise whenever the god comes close enough to be fully seen and experienced. In fact, the deeper meaning of "surrender" is, for Annamayya, precisely the attempt to put these contradictions back into the god in the context of playing with him. There is a cognitive act involved, one derived from the sheer fact of having a body with its always frustrated desires. The poet turns this frustration into god's problem; he has to solve the riddle he has posed.[85] Such surrender is a far cry from the theological notion of seeking refuge, *śaraṇâgati*. Here the mind is a complex whole, on one level infiltrated or informed by a divine aliveness, on another driven by residual, recalcitrant human needs.

> The god on the hill made your mind.
> Only you can make it think of him.
> The thoughts in your mind are partly god
> and partly you.
> Think him through.[86]

There is, apparently, a certain—perhaps rather limited—space for human volition in this ongoing conversation; an active subject (*kartā*—used here both for the god who made the mind and for the human being who can focus it in the direction he or she chooses) is involved in the intricate process of finding or knowing truth.

We have said "he or she" in line with our modern conventions, but, in fact, the speaking subject of the *adhyātma* poems is male. What is more, his very maleness seems to be part of the problem. A recurrent theme is the danger posed by women, especially since the desire they arouse is incapable of being satisfied.

> Wherever you go, wherever you are,
> the disease of desire has never been cured.
>
> When you put the compress of a woman's breasts
> on your aching body,
> the friction only makes things worse.
> The pain has never been cured.[87]

Out and out misogynistic statements are also not uncommon:

85. ACP 173, 2:242.
86. ACP 41, 1:168.
87. ACP 45, 1:183.

Listen, you gorgeous whores,
your seductive games won't work anymore.

You stole my mind as payment
and gave me the hell that is
your body. But I've mortgaged my mind
to the god. Your games
won't work any more.[88]

And so on. And yet this same poet composed many thousands of *śṛṅgāra* poems, for the most part in the feminine voice and almost always marked by exquisite sensitivity to a woman's feelings and desires.

7. Listening to the Padams (2): Erotic Verses

If we want to resolve this apparent contradiction, we need to pay closer attention to the way the love poems work. Take a striking example:

You tell him about subtlety.
If I insist, they'll say I'm too demanding.

Instead of talking back to me,
he would do better to send a messenger.
Why stare at me over and over?
He might bend his head, a little shy.

Tell him about subtlety.

Better than laughing so loudly,
he could be a little quiet.
Instead of pestering me to play,
let him simmer with some affection.

Tell him about subtlety.

Rather than tiring me by making love,
let him live quietly by my side.

88. ACP 17, 1:171.

I'm Alamelumanga. He's the god on the hill.
A loving touch would make all the difference.

Tell him about subtlety.[89]

The god's wife is speaking to her girlfriend with the thought that the latter will send a message to Veṅkaṭeśvara. Alamelumaṅga is somewhat exasperated with her husband's insensitivity. He talks too loud, laughs too loud, makes love too often, and, in general, seems to lack inner quiet. Worse, he has no empathic imagination for what a woman might want. Of course, she loves him: "a loving touch would make all the difference." An unspoken message from him would melt her, though she can hardly hope for this.

As we listen to the poem, we can easily forget that it was composed by a man. Its most conspicuous feature is the emphasis on subtlety. It should be sung or spoken in a woman's voice. One of the miracles of Annamayya's work is the way he has assimilated and found words for a rich range of female voices.

Not all of them are delicate and submissive. Quite often they are angry or upset, or at least start off so. As we saw in an earlier example, the mood changes as the poem progresses. The conflict, if there is one, usually ends in making love. Still, playful and sarcastic tones abound:

You don't have to tell me anymore lies.
Whatever you may have done,
did I ever argue with you?

You don't have to convince me.
Don't make promises.
What's eating you?
I never said anything.
Others have a lot to say,
but I never talk,

whatever you may have done.

Don't butter me up.
Cut out these fancy words.
I'm not one to nag you, but
I can't vouch for your family and friends,

whatever you may have done.[90]

89. SCP 419, 12:63.
90. SCP 341, 11:139.

Like the audacious tone that sometimes comes to the fore in the introspective *padams,* as we saw, a certain verbal abandon—aggressive and sardonic—comes through in many of the love-poems. What is, however, missing in the latter is the aspect of emotional torment and self-doubt. The *"śṛṅgāra"* speaker likes her body and is comfortable in it, including—or perhaps especially—its sexual mode. She seems never to lack confidence in her ability to deal with her partner (usually to come out on top) and to fulfill herself physically and emotionally. She is without guilt. Above all, she is close—as close as can be imagined—to the god himself, and not in a theoretical way. Such intimacy is not an idea but a reality.

This intimacy takes many forms; the sheer inventiveness of the erotic corpus is breathtaking. Poem after poem captures a singular moment in the ongoing love-relationship, which seems never to erode, never to become stereotyped. These are remarkable love-poems, creating vignettes nearly always imagined from a woman's vantage point. But they are also something more. We never forget who the male lover is. Thus, complex "theological" statements tend to surface in an implicit (sometimes explicit) manner, merging with the sensuous texture and context:

> This woman shows no signs
> of missing you, as if you'd never left.
> We wonder why.
>
> Thinking of you, seeing you
> inside herself, she embraces
> open space. Maybe she heard from someone
> that space is you.
>
> *She shows no signs of missing you.*
>
> She sings your praises, sees you take shape
> in her words, but she still wants more.
> She keeps staring at nothing.
> Somewhere she must have heard
> that you are everywhere.
>
> *She shows no signs of missing you.*
>
> Whenever she is with you, in thought or word,
> you're there, coupled with her.

They say you're alive in everything.
Now we know what they mean.

She shows no signs of missing you.[91]

Some external observer, probably a girlfriend of the heroine, is speaking to the god, reporting on her friend's behavior. The lover is absent, yet—in a rather unusual move for a *viraha* poem of separation—the beloved's hallucinatory behavior is interpreted as signifying this lover's actual presence. Every act has two meanings. The woman imagines her lover in the space before her and, spellbound by this delusion, stretches out her arms to embrace him, as in so many Indian love-poems. But the speaker interprets this move as actualizing a theological point: the god is everywhere; he is space itself. Nonetheless, the beloved "still wants more." It isn't quite enough to assert that god is everywhere. The interpretative series contains its own disjunction. A formal or theoretical level is exposed as masking a deeper emotional reality, strong enough to drive a woman mad.

Despite the apparent simplicity of style and structure, this poem is actually an exercise in double layering. On the surface, every negative has become a positive. Missing the lover is actually being with him, that is, realizing his presence. In a sense, this is the point of the entire endeavor, the driving urgency and aim of the poem. Beneath the surface, however, the speaker is actually delivering a veiled indictment of the god for mercilessly abandoning his beloved. The emotional reality of being alone or being left comes to dominate the rather superficial theological point precisely because of the disjunction between act and interpretation. This disjunction creates a space in which something new can happen, something between the god and those, like the lover, trying to reach him. In such a space, philosophical poses have, at best, an oblique and catalytic role.

Still, for all the irony emerging through the disjunction, the *padam* manages to culminate in the manner typical of the erotic poems—in genuine connectedness. "They say you're alive in everything." In a way, the poem goes beyond its own ironic undercurrent. The listener, following the buildup to the final verse and its refrain, does experience the god as alive in everything. Thus, our *padam* is, in fact, simultaneously a *śṛṅgāra* and an *adhyātma* poem, to use the conventional nomenclature; the latter aspect, perhaps a kind of Yoga or meditation, is no less real than the former, in terms of the

91. SCP 55, 6:61.

listener's experience. To make the point a little clearer, consider the way a classical text like the Sanskrit *Bhāgavata-purāṇa* consistently marshals precisely the same kind of argument that the speaker/interpreter makes here. When Krishna leaves the Gopīs behind in Vraj as he departs for Mathura, he explains to them that they need not feel this separation as real, since he is in truth "always with them," as God should be. Unfortunately, this somewhat self-serving explanation carries little weight with the Gopīs, who stand, forlorn, in the dust watching his chariot recede into the distance.[92] By contrast, Annamayya's *padam* makes the speaker's interpretation believable and convincing on a level accessible to anyone who can follow the deeper harmony implicit in the two competing tones. By the end, the god should, indeed, be present somewhere before, or within, the beloved, hence, also somewhere before, or within, the listener.

So what looks like an innocent love-poem opens up to reveal a more subtle and profound set of meanings. There is a reason for this conclusion. Both erotic and introspective poems appear to emerge from the same inner space, a space that is intensely occupied by a sense of the god in interaction with a rather open-ended, unfinished, changing subject. This space has a meditative, malleable quality. On the one hand, there is the fierce subjectivity that we saw so clearly in the *"adhyātma"* examples above. There the speaker seems to wish to empty himself out in order to make room for the god. On the other hand, the love-poems assume the god's true and compelling immediacy inside the self in a sensual and playful relation.

The two voices, or the two modes, clearly inhabit a single poet. They are also engaged with each other, sometimes spilling over from one category to the other.[93] A peculiar resonance is often discernible, reflecting what appears to be a serious and enduring tension. There is also an issue of perspective: from what vantage point, or what gender, is the poet relating to the god? The answer to this question also determines our place as listeners, overhearing the ongoing conversation within Annamayya. In the male mode, as we have seen, there is mostly conflict and disturbance; human life itself is burdened by a furious subjectivity, at war with the senses and the body. The vicissitudes of daily awareness, with its moods and cognitive puzzles, occupy the center of attention. In the female mode, almost infinitely elaborated,

92. *Bhāgavata-purāṇa* 10.39 and 10.47.

93. Some *padams* are ambiguously classified in the copper plates themselves; there are *śṛṅgāra padams* incorporated into the *adhyātma* plates and vice versa. For example, see ACP 159, 2:191 and 192; and ACP 160, 2:194, 195, and 196 (five *śṛṅgāra* poems recorded among the *adhyātma* set).

this same poet gives himself over to a harmonious and luxuriant erotic excess. In this state, "he" is even capable of controlling the god, demanding his attention, and enjoying his love. The listener cannot escape a clear-cut perception that the female, *śṛṅgāra* persona is somehow more fulfilling, indeed more full. Perhaps it is not by chance that Annamayya wrote four times as many *śṛṅgāra* poems as *adhyātma* poems. In his "female" self, he seems playful, happy, and complete. Maleness, with its tentative selfness, has receded or fallen away.

But in a wider view, this tension between male and female may give way to a resolution vested in the other, autonomous voice in the conversation, that of the intimately familiar god who absorbs and connects the two personae. As the introspective male, Annamayya offers his own moods and conflicts to the god in the hope that the latter will contain them for him. The entire inner screen of mentation, emotion, and confusion is what the poet can give to god. As the endlessly creative female, "he" actively draws the god into him and lives with him; each "*śṛṅgāra*" poem thus culminates in a total connection—physical or metaphysical. Perhaps most striking of all is the apparent ease of transition between these modes, as if the inner conversation flowed back and forth without impediment. There is every reason to believe that the poet composed in both modes throughout his life, moving from one to the other within a single day, giving each moment its own autonomy and integrity, as befits the compressed, vignette-like *padam* form.

There is a more consequential point to be made here. While each of the modes has its own clarity, Annamayya's originality may lie precisely in their surprising interdependence. We have suggested that the categorical division itself may reflect an attempt on the part of the poet's sons and their contemporaries to confine him to familiar genre-frames. (It is the fate of any truly great poet to be misunderstood in his own time.) In general, the *padams* are too complex to be captured by any simple label. Thus, the so-called *adhyātma* poems, with their confessional, agonized tones, often bear witness to the inadequacy of devotional surrender as a solution to the human predicament. Similarly, as we have said, the *śṛṅgāra* poems are far removed from classical courtly *śṛṅgāra* expressions of erotic love. In fact, Annamayya's massive "*śṛṅgāra*" corpus, with its almost infinite variations on the theme of sexual love, really embodies an entirely new type of love-poetry: nuanced, direct, inventive, bold, and intimate. That both modes end up projected onto Veṅkaṭeśvara speaks to the poet's own attempt to resolve the conflict between an extraordinary empathy for the subtleties of female emotion and a rooted deprecation of his own emotional and physical experience of himself. The god is thus a lover of women as well as an exemplar of potential dispassion. Most crucial of all is the sense of the new subjectivity and individual interiority that Annamayya opens up for his readers. It is this sensibility that may have been partly obscured by his sons in their rush to institutionalize their father's astonishing torrent of unconventional perception.

8. Padam Poetics

Before we end this introduction, we want to read one more poem with you. We have chosen one of the love-poems, which we will try to explore in its delicate shadings and tones:

ne nīku veru gānu nīvu nāk' ĕravu gāvu
ye nepamū veya nī pain iṇṭiki rāvayyā

cĕkkuna bĕṭṭina ceyi sesa vĕṭṭe nī mīda
mukku pai bĕṭṭina velu munde mĕccĕnu
vakkaṇal' aḍugan ela valaciti nāḍe nīku
yikkuvalu cĕppe gāni iṇṭiki rāvayyā

sigguvaḍḍa mogamuna sĕlavi navvulu regĕ
vĕggaliñcina kannule veḍuka jūcĕ
kaggi nīton aluganu kaḍu muddarālanu
yĕggul' emin ĕñcanu yiṇṭiki rāvayyā

vāḍina kemmovini vaḍi tenĕl' ūra joccĕ
vīḍina nĕrulalona virulu niṇḍĕ
yīḍane śrīveṅkaṭeśa yen alamelumaṅganu
yīḍugā gūḍitiv' ikan iṇṭiki rāvayyā

I'm no stranger to you.
You're not a borrowed thing.
I won't blame you anymore.
Come home.

I used to stare, my hand on my cheek.
Now that same hand welcomes you with flowers.
I would put my finger on my nose.
Now I like what you do.
Don't ask for promises.

I'm already in love.
I'll give you all my secrets.

Come home.

I was so shy. Now I smile for you.
The same eyes that couldn't hold you
now admire you.
I won't be cross with you anymore.
I'm your girl.
I'm not picky.

Come home.

My lips were parched.
Now they flow with honey.
My hair, once unkempt,
is now decked with flowers.
You're the god on the hill.
I'm Alamelumanga.
You're right for me.

Come home.[94]

The point of the departure is the woman's assertion of the already existing relationship. "I'm no stranger to you. You're not a borrowed thing." They are lovers who have, it seems, become estranged because of some accusations that *she* has made. Now all she wants is to get her lover back. She promises, "I won't blame you anymore." Then the plaintive, simple, direct refrain: "Come home."

She paints a complex, chronologically nuanced portrait of herself over several distinct stages. She begins with the immediate past, which must be fresh in his memory. There were days when they quarreled. Very cross with him, she would sulk, her cheek resting on her hand. Or she would hold her finger straight on her nose—a Telugu gesture to indicate extreme disapproval, used only in intimate contexts. She reminds him of these somewhat picturesque, if painful moments.

94. SCP 443, 12:145.

That stage is past. The same hand that held her face as she moped is now ready to scatter flowers before him. She has missed him terribly. For his part, it appears that he is negotiating, demanding that she promise not to find fault with him again. She reassures him, eluding the promise. She is already in love. She will no longer hold back: "I'll give you all my secrets" (*ikkuvalu*—a very concrete word, with a suggestion of opening up her secret parts).

The first stanza concludes at this point with the direct plea to him, "Come home,"—as if all words should really fall away before this one action, which will cut through everything. The *pallavi* refrain picks up the basic note, reminding him that they are already lovers.

Now we take a step farther back, to the early days of their meeting. She was an innocent girl, too shy even to look at her lover. She would turn her eyes away from him. All that has changed. She smiles at the thought of him. She wants to look at him openly and happily. Maybe a little too openly—she has to reassure him that she's not too aggressive. She's a *muddarālu,* an innocent woman, "his girl." We might conjecture that her excessive shyness was one of the reasons for his frustration with her, hence for the quarrel that got out of hand.

But it is important for her to let him know just how much she has suffered. Her lips are parched with longing, her hair unkempt. Today, anticipating his return, she has somehow transformed herself, made herself desirable—her lips will flow with honey, her hair is tied with flowers. Will he hear her and respond? She reminds him in the poem's culminating phrases that they are husband and wife; that he is Veṅkaṭeśvara, the god on the hill. She proudly speaks her own name: Alamelumaṅga. They are suited to each other; literally, he is right for her *(yīḍūgā gūḍitivi).* But there is an untranslatable pun, which also satisfies the requirement for a *śṛṅgāra* poem's finale: *k̲ūḍitivi* also means, "You've made love to me." Technically, if we take this meaning, he's already home. The process is complete by the time the poem reaches its final refrain.

And still she says, "Come home"—*iṇṭiki rāvayya*—as if this lover always has to come home, as if she were always waiting for him, hoping, as we also wait for him. The phrase binds the stanzas together each time it appears, weaving a garland of all these words. At the same time, this pregnant imperative intensifies with each repetition. Each time it is uttered, one hears a slightly different flourish, integrating what has just been said into the earlier pieces of text, so that these states and stages of their relationship become superimposed, like layers of memory flowing together in any living consciousness.

Similarly, the Telugu *pallavi—ne nīku veru gānu nīvu nāk' ĕravu gāvu,* "I'm no stranger to you./You're not a borrowed thing"—actually realizes itself literally as the poem proceeds. What begins as an assertion meant to remind the distant lover of past intimacy ends by expressing their renewed union. Separation has been relegated to the past; the song has truly brought the lovers together. Each time we hear the line, weaving the stanzas together, we recognize the transition that is in process. By the time the poem ends, this process is complete, and reality transformed. Language makes things happen.

The music of the poem has its own consistent progression. The first stanza is dominated by the harsh, head-rhyming, geminate unvoiced velar stop: *kk,* in line after line. The linguistic description sounds just like what it represents—you can still hear something of her distress. Her moping face may have been silent, but her feelings are hurt. The sounds she chooses makes this very clear. The second stanza shifts to somewhat softer sounds—the voiced velar stop *gg,* appropriate to her memories of their early meetings. By the last stanza, the ear is drenched in liquids (Telugu *ḍa* here is a *śithila-ḍakāra,* a soft retroflex much closer to *l* or *r* than a stop). When the speaker pronounces her own name, Alumelumaṅga, you can hear the syllables flowing smoothly into one another.

The text circles, or spirals, into a whole. Syntactically, the end feeds directly back into the beginning, but at a higher level. The absent lover has come close, and the distant god is now home.

This kind of poetry, and the supple form in which it is composed—including the aspect of musical performance—are something entirely new in Telugu. Extremely complex effects are achieved by an extreme economy of means. The transparent simplicity of the language should not blind us to its latent riches. One needs to hear these poems many times, preferably in live performance.

Annamayya was well aware of his originality. He regards his poetry as unprecedented and inimitable. He has nothing but bitter scorn for those who tried to imitate him:

> So you want to be poets, you idiots?
> Try basket weaving.
>
> ....
>
> You want to collect the betel I spit out,
> add a little camphor and chew it again?
> You steal my tune to fit your words.
> Won't god laugh you out of court?
>
> *Try basket weaving.*

You pick up the pits I throw away.
You feast on the crumbs I leave over.
Your hollow poetry, it's all fluff.
God has better taste than that.

Try basket weaving. . . .

What his imitators can steal is no more than the tune or "shadow" *(chāya)* of his achievement. Despite this note of censure, Annamayya's sons and grandsons went on composing *padams* in his style; indeed, a veritable *padam* industry developed at Tirupati along with the production of *śāstra*-like texts such as the *Saṅkīrtana-lakṣaṇamu* meant to provide a modicum of authority. A large and varied Tāḷḷapāka library was composed at Tirupati by Annamayya's wives, sons, grandsons, and others. Moreover, the *padam* form spread widely throughout south India in the centuries after Annamayya, attracting great poets such as Kṣetrayya in the seventeenth century and Sāraṅgapāṇi in the eighteenth.[95] Today the Annamayya corpus is still waiting to be studied, scientifically edited, and interpreted. But cassettes of *padams,* popularized by some of the best Carnatic performers, are now omnipresent. You can hear them most days while standing in line to see the god on the hill.

95. See Narayana Rao, Ramanujan, and Shulman, *When God Is a Customer,* passim.

Index of First Lines, Telugu

Index of First Lines, English